UNIVERSITY AT LAST!

In his sixties John took early retirement, gave up journalism and decided it was time to fulfil a life-long ambition to get himself an education. He had already taken A levels at night school, for fun, and found to his surprise that he had enough qualifications to become a full-time undergraduate at his home university — York. John describes the reactions of his wife, and the interactions of his fellow scholars, when instead of becoming an old age pensioner he became a student.

JOHN SCOTT

UNIVERSITY AT LAST!

Complete and Unabridged

ULVERSCROFT
Leicester

First published in Great Britain in 2010

First Large Print Edition
published 2012

The moral right of the author has been asserted

British Library CIP Data

Scott, John.
    University at last!
    1. Scott, John. 2. University of York- -Undergraduates- -
    Anecdotes. 3. Adult college students- -England- -York- -
    Anecdotes. 4. Retirees- -Education (Higher)- -England-
    -York- -Anecdotes. 5. Journalists- -Retirement-England-
    -York- -Anecdotes. 6. Large type books.
    I. Title
    378.1'98246'0942843–dc23

    ISBN 978–1–4448–1248–0

Published by
F. A. Thorpe (Publishing)
Anstey, Leicestershire

Set by Words & Graphics Ltd.
Anstey, Leicestershire
Printed and bound in Great Britain by
T. J. International Ltd., Padstow, Cornwall

This book is printed on acid-free paper

To Meriel,
for patiently putting up with it all . . .

1

'If you're not careful they'll turn you into their father confessor. They'll be all home-sick and lonely and want to cry on your shoulder. Always happens when there are older students around ... ' advised my daughter Penny, a former university student herself.

'Not when they are as old as I am,' I protested.

'I mean it.'

Meriel my wife shot me a stern look, 'And I mean it, too.'

So began an exciting adventure.

* * *

What should I wear?

I knew better than to put myself up for another homily by seeking the opinions of the women in my life. I did not want to resemble a retired bank manager, and neither did I want to look like one of the lecturers in their uniform of casual jacket and flannels; that really would be crossing the line. Jeans and trainers, maybe? No, I do not want the other students to think I am some ageing hippy flirting with his second childhood. I compromised with a V-neck sweater and tie under a blouson jacket.

After all the lazy timekeeping we had fallen into during retirement the family was back to early breakfasts again.

Meriel was unusually quiet while cooking the bacon. 'I know this is something you always wanted to do, but . . . '

'But what?'

'Going back to school at your age. I mean, why? I was glad to get out of the place.'

'It's not school. It's university.'

'Same thing. I take it you're not expecting me to see you off like this every day?'

I realised, with a jolt, that I have been rather self-centred about all this. Things might be changing for me, but not for Meriel. She was still doing the cooking and housekeeping and I would be disappearing as usual; as far as she was concerned I was back at work.

Adjustments would have to be made if this new student life of mine was not going to upset the marital harmony achieved after more than forty years. I was warily confident that this could be done.

I thought back to my retirement . . .

I read somewhere that the secret of a happy retirement was to do more things together. 'I'll come shopping with you,' I announced. 'I'll push the trolley and carry the heavy bags.'

I thought this was a chivalrous and manly thing to do, but surprisingly it was not received with much enthusiasm.

At the supermarket I was in another new world, which I approached with an open inquiring mind. I was intrigued by the design of the trolleys and their manoeuvrability. I was amazed by the selection of goods on display. I pondered how they coped with the replenishment of all the shelves . . .

'Try and keep up, John.'

Meriel was off down the corridors of commerce like a fox after a rabbit while I swerved and swirled dangerously in her wake. It was all right for her, being slim and nimble she could squeeze through gaps in the mass of shoppers at a speed no trolley could match. Time after time she got far ahead of me and I found her impatiently waving a packet of something.

'It's quicker to do it myself,' she complained. 'Now get yourself some cheese. It's over there.'

The cheese selections stretched from here to France. Which one should I try? I sniffed, probed and read the labels, some in French. Intrigued I started trying to translate.

An arm reached out from behind me. 'You like that and that. And you always said you wanted to try that. Oh, do come on!'

And, of course, I never packed the bags properly at the checkout. After three increasingly stress-laden supermarket visits Meriel asked, 'Why do you insist on coming with me to the supermarket? I'm quite capable of shopping by myself.'

'I'm trying to help.'

'You're not . . . '

A hurt silence followed.

'I love you dearly, John, but let me do the shopping. I've been doing it for years and I haven't starved you yet.'

★ ★ ★

In silence, Meriel served my first student breakfast. Yes indeed, more adjustments would most certainly have to be made.

I left home for my first day as a student in rather a low-key fashion. Not only was my family less than enthusiastic and encouraging, but this, for me, most important day in the rest of my life was overshadowed by the arrival of a BBC film unit who had hired my back garden and shed for a scene in a play. My send-off was muted as Meriel enthusiastically saw to their needs.

In a subdued mood I drove to college.

* * *

A nearby vehicle in the college car park had a sticker in the window: 'Of course I'm proud. I'm Norwegian.' This place was weird.

* * *

It was all rather nerve-racking. Ridiculously young students poured into the Central Hall on that first day, like a colony of ants on the move, and I was borne along by them as if I were some alien piece of flotsam.

Panic! There was not another tie in sight. Not even the Vice-Chancellor giving his welcome speech had chosen to wear one! Students wandered up on stage and gave confident little speeches about the different organisations we could join. What on earth was I, a grey-haired, sixty-five year old doing in this surging sea of vibrant youth?

It was all my father's fault, I concluded petulantly. If he had not chased after so many jobs in the bleak nineteen thirties I might have had a proper education at a more appropriate time in my life. Instead, I had been sent to eight different schools and had spectacularly failed my eleven plus examination, all of which had left me with a smouldering resentment that had lasted throughout my working life. On job application forms the academic qualifications section had always been accusingly, embarrassingly blank.

Why was I blaming my poor, dead father for my lack of education? They had been dark days back in the thirties and he had had a family to feed.

But then again, think of what I could have done with my life if I had been able to . . . Oh come on! Far too much water has gone under the bridge for those kinds of thoughts. *Carpe diem*, I told myself, seize the day, this day — now!

I was not sartorially isolated after all. Someone was approaching the rostrum wearing a tie and a smart suit; but they were being worn by the closely-cropped chairperson of the Students' Lesbian Society.

'Don't feel lonely and isolated out there,' she chirped. 'If you want friends, if you want support, we are here to help.'

What was I doing here!

The rest of the day was spent filling in

6

forms and getting registered. There was one cheerful note. I became a card carrying member of the Students' Union, which entitled me, among other concessions, to ten per cent off fish and chips sold in the nearby village. The card looked a little incongruous in my wallet alongside my pensioner's bus pass.

★　★　★

The cast and camera crews were still swarming around the garden dripping with self-importance and clutching clipboards when I returned. Here I was nervously entering an exciting new stage in my life, but clearly the play was the thing that really mattered.

'How did it go?' called Meriel from the midst of the throng.

'Fine,' I said, bursting to give details and share my new world.

'We've had a really exciting time here.'

'So did I.'

But my voice was lost in the throng.

2

Apart from an Elizabethan mansion, which the admin staff commandeered when the university was founded, the campus was brutally modern, yet softened by trees and lawns. I located my college: a gaunt, pebble-dashed, prefabricated structure landscaped into the side of a hill. As directed in the information pack, I headed for the notice boards. It reminded me of being in the army again anxiously searching for Part One Orders, to find out where I was going to be posted.

There was nothing on the notice board that concerned me, though my college postal pigeonhole was bulging with mail. I retreated to the cafeteria to sort it all out: invitations to join the Gay Society — thank you but no thank you; another to join the Mature Students Club — maybe; and a scattering of leaflets from other groups.

I was tempted by the Gilbert and Sullivan Society, and had momentary visions of wowing them as Poo Bah in the *Mikado* until common sense returned. Do not even think of embarrassing them by turning up for an audition, I told myself. But even so I felt a warm glow just reading all those invitations to do something. There was a buzz in the air here that was dangerously infectious.

Among all the invitations and leaflets there was a note from my personal supervisor summoning me to a meeting. Dr J seemed a gentle soul, sitting behind his desk in a room lined with shelves groaning beneath the weight of hundreds of books. All very impressive, but then, with typical journalistic cynicism I started wondering how he could possibly have read them all. Were they there just for show?

I had to stop this; I was not at work now. I really must not be so disparagingly critical about everyone and everything. I sensed he was uneasy, and on reflection I was not surprised: it was probably the first time that he had had a student nearly twice his age sitting before him.

★   ★   ★

Maybe he found it a bit embarrassing. He carefully explained that if I had any problems he was there to help. 'Are you concerned about any of the course work?'

'Yes.' One of the pre-university reading books was *The Green Knight*, which I had

9

discovered with horror was written in a foreign language, some weird tongue called Middle English.

'You will be given help with reading that,' he said when I explained my fears.

'But what did you think of the book?'

I had anticipated some questions might come up so I felt smugly prepared. 'I liked the description of the snow in the forest, the bit that goes, 'the snaw snittered snark . . . '' It was one of the few passages that I had managed to decipher with the help of the glossary at the end of the book.

'Ah! Yes,' said Dr J. He was out of his chair and striding towards the nearest book-lined wall. His fingers trailed along the shelves, selected a volume and then he riffled through the pages. 'Here it is: 'the snaw snittered snark . . . '' And off he went, dramatically reading the following lines in full declamatory mode. 'Wonderful stuff. You can feel the cold crackling in those lines can't you?'

I had to admit that it did sound rather grand even if not fully comprehensible. I looked on my personal supervisor in a new light. Perhaps he had read all those books on his shelves after all.

★　★　★

We were having our once-a-week, stately game of mixed doubles. 'I hope you're behaving yourself among all those girl students,' said Mike.

A few minutes later, he leapt to intercept a service return and the ball struck me hard in the lower regions. I sank to my knees and tried not to cry. The two ladies gathered round, sympathetic, but slightly giggly as women are apt to be at such moments on tennis courts.

Was this a cautionary lightning bolt from Olympus to remind me to behave myself in my new world?

★ ★ ★

I bore this in mind when I went to have my first meeting with my fellow students and to meet my first term tutor. There had been a long hunt down linoleum-clad corridors before I found the tutor's room, and there was no reply to my knock. What on earth would they think about having an old age pensioner in their midst? I was nervous.

Two girls drifted up: one a long-haired blonde with a casually self-assured air, and her friend who looked pale and frozen. She was clutching an A4 folder as if it were a hot water bottle. I later discovered Sarah was the

11

name of the pretty blonde and Kerry was her friend.

Before anything could be said by way of introduction a tall man came striding down the corridor, bouncing with energy. 'Aha! Students! Students! In! In! In!'

In we all went and no one seemed at all concerned about the old age pensioner. The study had books piled on every flat surface, desks, windowsills and chairs. These were cheerfully swept onto the floor or pushed to one side.

'Sit, sit, sit!'

Other students drifted in and the piles of books on the floor grew larger.

A lively, oriental girl bustled in, and pronounced her name twice so we would grasp it, 'I am Shu Lin, Shu Lin.'

Reading lists were distributed and our tutor Dr P addressed us in measured phrases, fingers pressed together in front of his chest he rocked back in his chair. 'To begin we will explore the relationships between the classical writers and those of the early English period: the odes of Horace with the poems of . . . '

Two boys tried to slither through the open door unnoticed. Dr P looked at them with all the pain of a first violinist interrupted in full flow. The explanatory lecture continued. We took away instructions to read three Greek plays and a Milton poem over the weekend. We were off! Here beginneth the learning. I felt commendably keen; life had a pleasurable purpose again.

The only trouble was that sitting down had become painful; I wished Mike had not hit me with that stupid tennis ball.

★ ★ ★

I attended my first lecture and joined a mass of students in the corridor outside the lecture room; they were all chattering and laughing. I stood there with my battered brief case, casual pullover and tie. A tie! For goodness sake, man, take it off! I did so quietly in a corner, feeling lonely and incongruous. Would anyone talk to me? Should I talk to them? Then two figures sidled up to me.

'Hi!' said Sarah. 'Have you read those Greek plays yet?'

'Sort of.' I did not want to sound too much like a swot.

'We had an away match, then the netball team had a party.'

'I think I've got flu.' Kerry clutched her A4 folder even more tightly. 'Just couldn't face any reading.'

We filed into the lecture hall and unbidden the two girls sat beside me. The lecturer was

13

my supervisor Dr J who seemed vaguely surprised at having such a large audience.

He drifted quietly into his opening remarks, 'If this lecture had a title, which it hasn't, it would be, 'What is poetry?'' He paused and looked around the hall. 'I don't propose to give you an answer.'

There was a ripple of unease. And then for some reason he wandered off into a discussion about brainwashing, saying it could not be done by lectures, but it could be done in seminars. 'In a seminar dissent can be spotted and coaxed out while still unformed and inarticulate so that it can be destroyed and discredited before it becomes a menace.'

This seemed terrifyingly lucid and it sent a frisson of concern through the hall. Why was this gentle tutor of poetry upsetting us with talk of brainwashing? Then he abruptly turned to the poems on the crib sheet and slowly picked them apart with such deftness and depth of understanding that the cold print started to sparkle with new meanings. Hello, hello, I am going to enjoy this.

★ ★ ★

At home I told Meriel, 'It's going to be really good. Those lecturers really know their stuff and we're doing some wonderful poems.'

'I'm glad you're enjoying it. You won't forget that the lawn needs cutting will you?'

★ ★ ★

I approached my first seminar with some trepidation, but also with a feeling of wary self-confidence. No one would brainwash me. Had I not emerged financially intact from a luncheon and seminar with a holiday time-share company? That really had been an attempt at brainwashing. Besides, I had never been frightened of speaking up in small groups. The family did not think that speaking up was going to be my problem — quite the contrary . . .

★ ★ ★

'You won't go on too much, will you?' said Meriel.

'I can't sit there looking dumb,' I protested. 'The whole idea is for us to talk.'

'Yes, but sometimes you don't know when to stop.'

'Oh thank you. You've never mentioned that before.'

'It didn't matter before.'

That was a blow to morale. Fortunately,

one does not have to live with someone for nearly forty years to know when the bottom lip is quivering while not outwardly moving.

'It could be different with students,' said Meriel gently. 'But remember that row you had with that clergyman at the coffee morning?'

'That was a discussion.'

'You might have thought so, but everyone else thought it was a row.'

The clergyman had irritated me by saying that the miracles and much else in the Bible were symbolic — 'Attempts to put into words things, which were inexpressible.' To which I had said, 'If God is God why can't you accept that His Son could do miracles?' He had replied, I thought pompously, 'God does not work that way.' Admittedly after that the discussion had got somewhat heated.

'All I ask,' Meriel continued, 'is that you don't start wagging your finger at them like you did then.'

'Did I wag my finger at him?'

'You most certainly did.'

I was reduced to thoughtful contemplation, which was obviously the sole purpose for bringing up the subject.

★   ★   ★

We had been presented with a booklet of 'do's and don'ts' for seminars. At first glance it appeared to be mainly about jotting down ideas and finding suitable gaps in the discussion to put them across; how to express oneself; how to disagree without being nasty about it. There was quite a bit about not permitting power blocks to develop. What was going on in this university? Then I noticed that mature students had been singled out for a chapter to themselves.

'Mature students can consider themselves under pressure because, being more fluent and experienced, they feel more is expected from them.'

I didn't think that. These young kids were fresh out of school and knew far more about poetry and plays than I did. They had brains like sponges that sucked in information and the fluency of some of them was terrifying. All right, I had the older person's confidence to speak up without too much embarrass-ment, but the problem was knowing what to speak up about. My worry was that I would fluently and confidently betray my ignorance every time I opened my mouth.

I also feared making them embarrassed. The ones I had met so far were all decent, young people, the sort of nicely brought up youngsters who had been taught to be polite to their elders. I could just imagine them thinking, 'How can we stop this poor old gentleman putting his foot in it again without upsetting him?'

★ ★ ★

Zorica and I had to do a presentation comparing Juvenal the Roman Satirist and Dr Johnson. Zorica was round, plump and pretty, with dark eyes and a cascade of brown curly hair. She volunteered for Johnson, but confessed that she had only read one of the two required poems. Ah well, I was not her keeper. Fortunately I had read Juvenal before as part of a failed attempt to write a best-selling novel set in Roman times.

★ ★ ★

There was a palpable tension on the faces gathered around the table in the seminar room. No one could hide here and everyone was studying notes for their individual presentations. Dr P burst into the room and swung his briefcase onto the table with a thud. 'Break out the Falernian wine,' he cried.

This was an echo from his lecture on Horace and the pastoral mode, but his

18

cheerfulness failed to still the nervousness in the air.

It all started slowly with a paper by two of the girls on Greek tragedy and divine intervention. It was one of my pet subjects for pontificating, but I bit my tongue.

Dr P was low key and encouraging.

It was our turn. I launched into Juvenal, calling him Rome's tabloid scandalmonger. People started grinning and the old ham arose within me and I started enjoying myself.

Oh for goodness sake, stop it! I had slipped into Women's Institute chat mode! Even Dr P was grinning. I quickly handed over to Zorica.

She reeled off some quotes and opinions about Johnson with the confidence of one who had known him intimately. Never believe a student who says she or he has not done their homework. The conversation took off and rocketed around the table.

One girl asked a question about Juvenal. To my horror I found myself answering her. Dr P did not even raise an eyebrow. As an act of contrition and apology I fell silent — for at least ten minutes.

Two hours passed. I walked out of my first seminar feeling that my brain had been in overdrive.

'Well done, you,' said the lady I met at the party. 'A full time student, eh? Marvellous!'

A hard-eyed businessman was staring hard at me and twirling his wine glass impatiently. 'Quite a lot of competition to get into that university, I believe.'

'One in ten acceptance rate,' I replied sensing hostility.

'Come across any resentment, have you? I presume you must have kept someone out, someone younger?'

'You apply and they choose,' I said. 'And I had all the necessary academic qualifications.'

'Yes, but you had your chance years ago, didn't you? Shouldn't you be letting the young ones have a go now, not squeezing them out?'

'I was not lucky enough to have the opportunity when I was young.'

Before I could say any more the lady came to my rescue with all the fierceness of Boadicea in her chariot. 'Typical ageism thinking,' she snapped. 'You are assuming quite wrongly that older people have nothing to contribute to society.'

'Indeed?' The man was startled to find himself attacked on the flank while he thought he was only needling me.

'Yes, quite wrong,' repeated the lady. 'A late education can not only benefit older people, but it can benefit society enormously in many ways. Ask any university lecturer and he'll tell you that mature students help the younger ones. With their greater experience of the world they can bring greater depth to discussions.'

'Oh really' said the business man.

'Yes, oh really,' said the woman and there was the merest flicker of a wink at me.

'Quite so,' I said.

Faced with a war on two fronts the businessman spotted someone else to whom he urgently needed to talk.

'Pompous idiot,' said my smartly dressed and impressively eloquent defender. 'What does he know about it?'

'I appreciate your help.'

'Couldn't let that go by. I got my higher degree when I was fifty. So I know something about it. Good luck to you.'

Despite her gallant defence that blasted man had managed to splash acid all over my nice, new ivory tower.

3

Anna laid a hand dramatically on my arm. 'John, I want your advice.'

A dazzling, Mediterranean beauty was asking for my advice. Warning bells rang loud and clear, but secretly I felt flattered.

'This is Richard by the way,' said Anna. 'We'll bring our coffee over.'

A tall young man gave me a shy grin. It was changeover time for lectures and the cafeteria was packed. I shuffled along in the coffee queue and we took our trays to a less crowded part of the room. Anna, with Richard quietly in attendance, sat beside me.

'Have you,' she looked back over her shoulder with all the wariness of a Guy Fawkes conspirator, 'have you met David S?'

I shook my head.

'He's my tutor and he's weird. He just stares at me. I don't know if he fancies me or what, but he picks up on everything I say and criticises it. I can't stand a whole term with him. Can't! Won't! What do you think I should do?'

I was aware that Richard was watching me closely.

'What do you think, Richard?' I asked

He shrugged his shoulders and pursed his lips.

'I just don't get on with him,' Anna said ignoring the interruption. 'I'm dreading what he's going to say about my first essay. It's keeping me awake just thinking about it.'

'Why not give it a bit more time,' I suggested.

'Do you think so?'

'Perhaps you're being a bit over-sensitive.'

'That's what Richard says! Do you think I am being over-sensitive? Perhaps I am.' She lit a cigarette with a grand, Garbo flourish. 'He makes me so angry!'

'It'll sort itself out,' Richard was full of Anglo-Saxon reasonableness.

'It's all right for him,' said Anna. Again she laid a hand on my arm.

I wished she would not do that.

'This one's brilliant,' she said, nodding at her companion. 'Straight A's for all his essays. Sure-fire starred First. It's me that's struggling.'

Richard has gone slightly red. 'You're not struggling. You're doing great.'

But Anna is back to me. 'So what if this weirdo doesn't alter?'

Words kept repeating themselves in my head: don't get involved, Dad! 'You'll have to see your supervisor. That's what he's there for.' That advice I thought was safe enough.

'I suppose so.' She drew heavily on her cigarette and blew out a voluminous smoke cloud.

There was a long silence.

I think I should explain a little more about Anna. Her father was a Spanish speaking South American diplomat living in Italy with his Italian wife; their daughter, Anna, was therefore fluent in Spanish, Italian, French, German and English. The good fairy at her christening had also thrown in film star good looks, and a high intelligence. Despite all these blessings she was firmly convinced that the whole world was conspiring against her for some reason or another.

So what, I told myself? It was not my problem. She was a big girl. I drank my coffee and escaped.

★   ★   ★

Warily I told Meriel about the encounter.

'Penny warned you. Pretty girl is she?'

'What's that got to do with it?'

'Hah!'

Unfortunately this discussion had just preceded me collecting all my lectures and seminars into a list, which I had presented to Meriel.

'What's this for?' she had asked.

'So you know when I am coming and going.'

'Why do I need to know that?

'I just thought you would like to know.'

'Fine,' she said, 'as long as you don't expect to find me waiting here with the kettle boiling and administrating tea and sympathy at all hours.'

There was something in the air and as I drove to the university I pondered this shadow over my happy landscape. And Meriel was right as usual. I was expecting her to run a comfortable B&B for my personal convenience while I wallowed in fresh fields and pastures new. And talking of fresh fields I suddenly remembered that, despite having been reminded, I had forgotten yet again to cut the lawn. And while I was in worrying mode, I wished that ache in my groin would go away.

★ ★ ★

The mysteries of structuralism and even post-structuralism were to be explained to us in a lecture on literary criticism. I approached the session with hostile intent; I instinctively hated big words that I could not understand. Sarah and Kerry appeared at my elbows, as everyone clattered into the rows of desks.

The lecturer was a middle-aged lady with the intelligent homely look of a head librarian. 'With literature, we must step back and ask a series of questions and then get behind the questions we are asking.'

Oh yes. I was concentrating hard, determined to try and make sense of something I feared would be obtuse. She gave us the analogy of six blind men touching an elephant and each coming up with a different description of the beast. OK I could see that even if they could not: different people saw things in different ways.

'Write this down.'

Pens were seized.

'Behind every statement about poetry there is an explicit theory. There is no completely neutral approach. It is all based on a network of assumptions, which critical theory attempts to uncover.'

Wow, this was getting deep. It made more sense when I deciphered my shorthand note sometime later, but at the time confusion was building. On we went. 'Naturally, we have learned to approach a text using common-sense, but that commonsense could have become naturalised.'

Naturalised? The use of that word in that context puzzled me.

She quoted Freud on women's place in society, 'A quote, which,' she said, 'was accepted as natural and commonsense at the time.'

OK yes, I had got that now: what we regarded as commonsense could change. From that she concluded that we should therefore always 'problematise' such statements.

I rebelled at the word problematise! I had spent my whole working life trying to simplify and explain, and now I was being asked to 'problematise'.

In my indignation I lost track of this closely-reasoned lecture completely, and when my concentration returned she was discussing a famous literary don who she said was 'anti theory'.

Sensible man, was my instinctive reaction.

But then the poor don was accused of making the tacit assumption that there was such a thing as a universally intelligent reader, someone for whom he had drawn up an essential order of English poetry as seen as a whole. This clearly did not fit in with the good lady's 'problematise-your-questions' approach. Now I was irritated. Clearly, what was being aired here was an ongoing spat in the rarefied upper layers of learning on how to approach English literature.

I was desperately trying to grasp and simplify what I was being told. I concluded that the don was under fire, because not all of his peers agreed with the pecking order that he had chosen for English literature, nor did they like the theories and assumptions that had driven his selection. If all this were so, then the ground was shifting under my feet. Here we were, poor, simplistic students, naively expecting our lecturers to put before us for study the very best that English literature could offer. But if I had understood correctly, the experts could not agree among themselves what was the best. Worse still they could not even settle on a method for choosing what was the best. They were still one step back busily 'problematising' and getting behind the assumptions behind their own questions before they could tackle the actual literature . . .

Please, please, enough! Do not confuse me! Just tell me what books I should read and I will read them.

Weird images started to circulate in my poor, tired, brain: was our lecturer suggesting that one of those six blind men feeling their way round the elephant was the famous don in question?

In which case had the poor man got hold of the beast's tail or its trunk? I had to stop this confused meandering before madness set in.

Kerry was sitting beside me writing energetically — line after line, neat and closely packed. I was impressed and then alarmed at my lack of understanding.

I glanced across to see what she was recording that I had clearly missed. On top of her A4 pad I read, 'Dear Mum and Dad'.

* * *

Round and round on the word processor went my first essay. Meriel realised that university matters had become serious and was very understanding. She laid cups of tea outside the study door, but I was so absorbed in what I was doing that many of them went cold. Guiltily, I secretly poured them down the toilet.

At lunchtime came the call, 'Come down when you're ready and I'll make the tea.'

An hour later, there was a gentle tap on the door. 'Shouldn't you have a break?'

'Good grief! Is it that time?'

If more was expected from a mature student in seminars, then what was expected from one who wrote for a living? I knew there was an inbuilt academic hostility towards all things journalistic. I remembered a leading academic gleefully recalling his encounter with a tabloid journalist. The reporter had asked him to expand on some new teaching practice and had foolishly asked him to think and express himself in headlines.

'So I told him,' said the professor smugly, 'I want to teach my students *not* to think and express themselves in headlines.'

I pitied the humiliation of that poor reporter. I knew what he had been after, he wanted something, which he feared would be obtuse to be clearly and simply expressed for his readers. What was wrong with that? Sometimes thinking in headlines focussed the mind and provided a welcome glimpse of clarity.

So what was I doing with this essay? My brain never went round and round like this when I was working; I just wrote the stuff and sent it. Despite my scepticism I found myself questioning and 'problematising' everything. There was that blasted word again. My poor critical judgement and profound lack of knowledge would be laid before my masters, neatly typed in reasonably good English and clear for all to see. I was not 'into' learned obtuseness.

Meriel's eyes had been glazing over during dinner as I kept her up to date with my day's studies. 'You won't forget to put the dustbins out tomorrow, will you?'

I failed to find the link between dustbins and my views on Greek tragedy, but clearly there was one as far as she was concerned.

4

There was news from Hampshire: daughter Penny was expecting a baby. What a tumult of emotions! If the Good Lord pleased, we were going to be grandparents!

A feeling of anxiety predominated. We had lost our first child, a boy, stillborn. That one word, stillborn, in a newspaper birth announcement encapsulated so much sadness and so many dashed dreams.

I remembered that I had been sent to a dark little office at the back of the hospital to sign a lot of forms. This very good firm in the town would look after everything, they told me, including the burial. I tried and failed to push a stream of dreadful images out of my mind.

Please, please do not let my daughter go through a trauma like that.

★ ★ ★

I was back in the swing of lectures and seminars. The university corridors were becoming more familiar and the number of faces I knew was growing. After one of the lectures Anna joined me for coffee, but without the boyfriend who was in a seminar.

'What do you think of Richard?' she enthused. 'Isn't he brilliant!' Not waiting for a reply she added, 'But he's not really assertive enough, you know. I'm going to have to work on him.'

I was amused by this female moulding of a potential mate. 'How did you meet him?' That was not getting involved, was it? It was just polite, natural curiosity, surely?

'I just saw him.'

'You saw him? Don't you mean he just saw you?' Oh, John how naive and out of touch you are with today's young.

'No, I saw him,' Anna was momentarily puzzled at my interruption. 'I thought, 'He's gorgeous!' So I kept dropping into his room for coffee. He got the message — eventually.'

I shook my head and laughed. Lucky old Richard! That sort of thing never happened in my day. In my world girls never chased boys, and if they did it was done so subtly that I was never aware of it.

Anna meanwhile wanted to talk and I was very happy to listen. 'There are not that many good looking boys around, so there's lots of competition among the girls. Richard was engaged you know.'

'Was?'

'Yes. After I went out with him a couple of times his fiancée came down for the weekend. Went back in tears.'

Anna tapped her cigarette ash into her saucer and flicked back the long dark hair.

'Oh dear.'

'His choice. Very weepy scene at the railway station, I gather.' She pursed her lips and dismissed the ex-fiancée with a shrug of the shoulders.

Oh, the ruthlessness of maidens in love. I thought I should tactfully change the subject. 'How are you getting on with your troublesome tutor?'

The reply was similarly dismissive. 'He's fine. He gave me a very good mark for my essay.'

Anna looked at her watch, remembered another appointment, and was away. Ah, the ephemeral troubles of the young, but, thinking about troubles, that nagging ache in my groin had not gone away.

★ ★ ★

'I'm worried about you,' said Meriel. 'I've booked an appointment for you at the doctor's. You've complained about that pain long enough. And while you are about it, ask him if you should be playing tennis at your age.'

34

We had to learn Anglo-Saxon! I went to university to read English not foreign languages, but part of the English course involves literature in a foreign tongue. One option is Anglo-Saxon. The tutor looked like a Nordic warrior: six foot four, fair hair and blue eyes. The girl students had that mesmerised look that never passed over any female in my presence.

Grudgingly, I conceded that I was in the presence of a teaching genius.

A piece of gobbledegook was put before us on the blackboard. We were invited to pick out words that looked familiar. He wrote them on another blackboard suggesting associations with English words we knew. We intoned phrases under his guidance and they, too, sounded familiar. A collective light dawned: we were looking at the Lord's Prayer in Anglo-Saxon.

Two hours later the seminar broke up, gently bubbling with excitement. Most of the girls decided to do Anglo-Saxon as the foreign language element of their degree. I was impressed, but not that impressed. My poor brain would rather expand on the little French that it knew rather than the Anglo-Saxon which it knew not.

★ ★ ★

Shu Lin's expensive CD equipment was on full power in her study. It was next door to our tutor's office, so her room had become the waiting room for tutorials. Shu Lin, I learned, had worked on radio stations and newspapers in Thailand and was studying politics as well as English. She was obviously very bright, a future politician or Far Eastern revolutionary in the making, perhaps.

Dr P stuck his head round the door. 'All very civilised in here . . . What's the music?'

'Faust,' said Shu Lin.

'Very appropriate for Milton,' he said.

As usual in this tutorial group Mary, our leading exponent of 'grunge' fashion, tried to get the conversation around to Renaissance architecture and painting in foreign lands. She kept trying to lure Dr P into some Florentine art gallery, which he clearly knew well, but he valiantly kept leading her back to Milton. When I handed in my first essay, typed on the home word processor and pristine in a plastic envelope, Dr P was ecstatic. 'How wonderful! It is typed. Marvellous!'

I was embarrassed.

'Get thee to a typewriter,' Dr P told the girls.

They protested heatedly that they could not type.

'For goodness sake, the university will teach you how to type for nothing, and how to use a word processor. Get yourselves computerised. Get digitalised!'

I had made my tutor happy with my first essay, but he had not read the darned thing yet.

★ ★ ★

We all filed in for yet another lecture: the Bible's place in English literature. Ho hum! Kerry was alone, apart from her A4 file, and Sarah entered with a boyfriend in tow. The pairing off had started. Harry, my lecturer friend, had warned me this would happen. And then look out for fireworks, he said.

The bearded lecturer looked like the prophet Isaiah in a tweed jacket. He waited until we had settled and then suddenly, coming out of the loudspeakers, the room was flooded with the sound of the opening of Haydn's *Creation*.

'Out of the chaos of discordant sounds,' cried our lecturer above the music, and then he started reciting in a foreign tongue. 'Don't worry if you don't understand German,' he interjected as the music crashed around us.

37

We were all intrigued. Had we at last come face to face with a mad professor?

There were more dramatic, incomprehensible recitations in German, and then abruptly he uttered a wild yell to coincide with the climax of the music. Everyone jumped.

'That was in C Major. The chord, which represents the Creation, the Word! Let there be light!' He had our total concentration.

Kerry was open mouthed.

What would he do for an encore?

We cantered jokily through the Bible's account of the Creation and reached David dancing before the Ark of the Covenant.

'Lifting up his skirts, he was, and showing off his legs. His wife didn't like it a bit. So David told her it was the Lord's work and the Bible says, 'She had no children'.' The lecturer looked at us all archly. 'Obviously, after this incident marital relations were suspended. In other words: no more nooky.'

The lecture hall exploded into laughter. There was more to the Bible than first met the eye. Very clever, but I wondered how many of his young audience would be intrigued enough to delve into the Good Book themselves.

★ ★ ★

38

At one of the more crowded lectures a bouncy black girl with long, finely plaited dreadlocks interwoven with beads squeezed in beside me. 'Hi! Where you from?'

It was the first time that anyone had taken any interest in my presence. 'Local.'

She was in her early twenties, with an easy air of self-confidence and friendliness. 'Enjoying it?'

'Very much.'

'London, me.' She slipped into a Caribbean accent. 'My name's Tanya, man, parents from Jamaica, but me — pure cockney.' She laughed, sending her dreadlocks swaying.

I was intrigued by their length and the fineness of the plaiting. She saw me looking at them and gave her head a shake that made the beads rattle.

'It must take you ages doing them up.'

Tanya smoothed one of the shorter braids with her fingers and gave it a quick tug. It came away in her hand.

'You buy 'em, and weave 'em in. Saves a lot of time. Very useful. Want some?' Cheekily she looked at my bald head and grinned broadly.

The lecturer was making his way to the podium.

'Not really interested in this,' she said. 'Did this play at A level. Just wanted to pick up a bit more info for an essay. Did you do A levels?'

Did I do A levels! How did the girl think I got into the university? Bribery? 'I most certainly did. I took three of them, got an A and two B's.'

But before I could boast any further the lecturer was shuffling his notes. Did I take A levels indeed!

★ ★ ★

The lecture was boring and I started to reminisce about my A levels — all those winter evenings hurrying through dinner and going off to night school and doing homework at weekends. And then there was the incredulity of work colleagues, summed up succinctly in the phrase: why for Heaven's sake? Why not, I said? Some of them studied photography, some even went to painting classes; I preferred to do something a bit more academic. There was a reason: one which I kept to myself. The resentment still smouldered. I wanted to prove that I might have done a bit more all those years ago, if only . . .

And then I remembered something else about those A levels — how they had created an unexpected and potentially serious domestic problem.

40

I had enrolled at night school in the September and, without any serious forethought, had put my name down for the exams in the following year. Only later did it dawn on me that the exam dates coincided with our summer holiday in Cornwall: an event booked, fixed and carved in stone. When the clash was discovered it was made very clear what came first. A whole term's study would have to be aborted — until the nice night-school teacher came up with an idea.

'I'll write to Penzance Grammar school,' she said. 'See if they can help.' And to my surprise they could. At long range I was formally enrolled as one of their pupils; I was told I could take the exam alongside their scholars.

So I sunbathed on the beach at St Ives and swotted at my books before driving along the peninsula to Penzance Grammar School; there I presented myself and my passport, for identification purposes, to the headmaster. He thought it was all very amusing but his mood was not shared by the invigilator in the exam room; he was totally unsmiling.

I sat at my allotted desk surrounded by fresh-faced pupils, many of whom eyed me shyly. Carefully, I unwrapped three mints and laid them out, still on their wrappers, along the edge of my desk; they were a refreshing cure for a dry mouth. But the invigilator watching me from afar was clearly suspicious. As the exam progressed he circled the desks and eventually approached, crab-wise. He stopped behind me and I realised that he was reading my mint wrappers. He must have thought I was trying to smuggle in the answers. I forgave my unsmiling invigilator when he announced time was up.

A girl at one of the desks near me was clearly distressed and went on writing. He repeated that the exam was over, but she went on scribbling furiously. With everyone watching he went up to her, knelt by her desk, and spoke to her in a whisper. The girl flung down her pen and burst into tears. The invigilator beckoned with his hand that we should all leave and we sidled out; he stayed, talking to her quietly.

At that moment the seriousness of it all hit me. For me, lying on the beach sunbathing and pretentiously reading school books, it was a self-indulgent bit of fun. What did it matter for me? But for these youngsters, they had just undergone a crucial test the result of which could change the whole course of their lives. Suddenly I felt guilty; I was an intruder in a vulnerable, young persons' world. I went back to the sun, sea and sand, feeling humble and subdued.

I dragged my thoughts back from St Ives to the lecturer who was still droning on up on the rostrum. Oh yes, I had most certainly taken A levels.

5

Winter was upon us. The wind howled across the campus footbridge. We all scurried through the colleges eager to reach our destinations under cover. It was damp and miserable and I had a cold and a cough. Lectures were marathons of choking frustration. My brief case was full of sweets and lozenges and I tried to time my coughs with the breaks in sentences.

You've never been well since you went to that university, was Meriel's opinion. I blamed a virile strain of germs incubated by the young, but she was not amused.

Everyone was coughing. At Dr P's tutorial we were all spluttering and he eyed us distastefully. He wanted us to read out loud portions of *Paradise Lost*: 'So you can understand something of the grandeur, the power of it.' And here I was operating on half a lung.

He set me off reading a long passage, which had no discernible full stops. I ran out of breath in mid-phrase to everyone's amusement.

Dr P took over, waving one hand in the air

and singing out the lines in a ringing baritone. I had a sudden childhood memory of a Welsh preacher, arms raised, fervently crying the Word of God from the pulpit of the Congregational Chapel in Pwllheli.

Dr P however knew when he was no longer holding his audience's attention. He snapped shut his book. 'The best thing you lot can do is get yourselves to bed.'

⋆   ⋆   ⋆

At the doctor's I explained: 'I got hit down here with a tennis ball.' I liked Dr M; every time I had approached him with sprained ankles, pulled muscles and tennis elbows he had joked about young men's injuries. But he was not joking now. He was very gentle with his rubber gloved hands, but it still hurt.

'We'd better have you to a specialist,' he said.

Perhaps it was because I had read too much Greek tragedy, but I never subscribed to the cheerful, 'every cloud has a silver lining' attitude to life. Quite the opposite. I had been convinced for a long time that every blue sky had a rain cloud lurking in it somewhere. When everything in life seemed to be going well that was the moment to look over your shoulder and start worrying.

I got that sick feeling in the pit of the stomach just like that time when Meriel found that lump. That, too, had come about when life was sweet and we had a toddler enriching our lives; we faced dark thoughts of what might happen, but thank the Good Lord it did not. And now we had this . . .

★ ★ ★

Apart from Tanya the students never batted an eyelid at my presence. I was just there and they showed no curiosity as to why. Through Richard and Anna I met one of their friends, Julien, who regularly entertained the three of us to tea in his rooms after seminar sessions. Tall, thin and serious, he carefully weighed all his words and appeared very grownup indeed. His fellow students must have thought so, too, for he had been elected as their representative on the academic board.

The after-seminar tea breaks in his room were my introduction into real student life. We drank milky tea out of grimy mugs; there were plastic bags of vegetables on the floor, dirty cooking pots in the sink and weird posters on the walls. Anna held court complaining loudly about the courses and about yet another tutor who did not understand her. Richard just grinned, but

46

Julien, a born lawyer, always tried to put a counter point of view.

'Julien,' said Anna sharply, 'I'm not arguing about this. Just accept it from me; the man is a moron.'

Julien shrugged his shoulders and stirred dried milk into the mugs of tea. I had the place of honour, the only armchair, so I sat back, listened and enjoyed it. Was this the stuff that would make up their campus memories? They did not really want to hear my views so I rarely gave them. Once again my role in life was to listen. When my opinion was sought I usually asked what they thought and nodded my head at what I considered to be the soundest answer. It was a conversational system that appeared to work. They were quick, lively, highly articulate and fun to be with.

I was becoming more and more aware of the appalling gaps in my general English education. I went hunting for a poem by Jonson — 'Oh rare Ben Jonson,' I said smugly to myself. But I could not find the poem under his name on the library computer. This was ridiculous! Eventually I realised that I was spelling Ben Jonson with an H and confusing him with the worthy doctor.

Meriel looked at me aghast. 'Even I knew that.'

Another good reason not to say too much in seminars.

★ ★ ★

But now I could be claiming to be doing some serious research. I had to find villages and towns whose names revealed their Anglo-Saxon origins. This was a cunning ploy by our charismatic Anglo-Saxon teacher to make the language relevant to our time. The librarians were as helpful as ever by guiding me to the right books, a task made easier for them, I'm sure, by the stream of scholars who had travelled this path before me.

In the books I found the city of Nottingham and I was intrigued to read that there was once an Anglo-Saxon chief called Snot. I had a quiet snigger about this and then found that his people, or 'ings', lived with him in a 'ham' or village: so Snot's-ings-ham became the name of the place where Snot's people lived: Snottingham, Nottingham. I had a childish sense of achievement at this discovery. Who was a clever teacher, then!

With all the books, the lectures and the searches through the library shelves, I became lost in a happily satisfying world. And then one day, while reading peacefully in the library, something urgently triggered me to look at my watch. It was an almost panic-driven need to know the time, as if I had forgotten something vitally important. It was four o'clock and as I stared at my watch I realised what had happened. My body clock had gone back to its old work schedules. It was time for the daily news list to go through, always a time of tension in the office. But now I watched the minutes tick past four o'clock. That deadline no longer existed. I really was in another world.

★ ★ ★

My first essay was returned. I took it back to the car, like a worried schoolboy wanting to be either elated or deflated in private. I had got an A minus! But what shame! Sprinklings of spelling mistakes had all been neatly underlined. I really must get a spellchecker on my computer, or would that be cheating?

With a spring in my step I headed for one of Dr P's tutorials. We were to discuss Lovelace's *The Grasshopper*, but someone mentioned Gilbert and Sullivan and the current university production of *Patience*. I knew this opera well, so I happily threw in the quote: 'Greenery-yallery, Grosvenor Gallery.' Dr P burst into song and gave us chorus and verse. We all reluctantly got back to *The*

Grasshopper and then Dr P felt we should also hear an ancient ode, which expressed the same sentiments. He read it out to us, in Latin. 'Magnificent is it not?'

I did not have the courage to admit that I did not learn Latin at any of the eight schools I had attended, though in deference to his opinion I did make a note to look up the ode, in English. It was worrying. These gaps in my formal education kept yawning.

Other students, I discovered, had clearly benefited from a classical education for a much higher standard of graffiti was on display in the toilets, e.g. Oedipus — your mother rang. And current affairs were not forgotten. On another wall someone solicited support for the IRA men imprisoned for the Guildford bombing. What about the Guildford Four? they said, to which someone had replied, What about the Renault Five?

★   ★   ★

I hate hearty surgeons. They are so determinedly cheerful. This one stood over me wearing his surgical mask and with rubber-clad hands raised. I was lying on a trolley like a joint of pork awaiting the carving knife. 'Your little problem hasn't vanished in the night, has it?'

50

I assured him that his butchery skills were still required and that he would not be done out of his fees.

'Let's have a look,' he whisked the sheet away. Surgeon and nurses had a long stare.

'Count to ten,' said the anaesthetist, but, of course, I could not. I am told that no one ever can, so why do they damn well ask? Sorry to be swearing, but really!

All was well. Everything had been straightforward and normal. Nothing unpleasant had been found. The relief was enormous. I reminded myself of the promise I had made that I would never again worry about trivial things, if only this particular shadow could be removed from my life. That shadow had gone and I could count my blessings and get on with living.

But how quickly one forgets. Now I was brooding about something else, something which kept me awake in the wee small hours.

Under the influence of the anaesthetic there had been a complete blank in my life between my chat in the antechamber of the operating theatre and my reawakening in the ward some two hours later. Even when fast asleep I always felt I was 'still there,' dreaming or at least subconsciously aware that I could immediately awake if, say, the telephone rang. But two hours of my life had been lost in complete oblivion, an empty, dreamless nothingness. I had been switched off. I stared at the bedroom ceiling in the semidarkness and I wondered if that was what 'it' would be like. The light would just go out and then nothing . . .

Oh, for goodness sake, come on! Creep downstairs, make yourself a cup of tea and pull yourself together. That darned university was making me think too much.

6

Lectures came and went and faces became more familiar, though I was still part of a group, which involved Anna, Richard and Julien. A camaraderie built up created by the tensions of essays and seminar presentations, and in the library friendly young faces nodded from behind books

I enjoyed the calm, friendly, purposeful world. Julien continued to dispense tea and talk in his room, and Anna and Richard seemed very content with each other. He was collecting straight A's for all his essays, but grinned sheepishly whenever it was mentioned. Anna was still convinced that the world thought her foreign and inarticulate. Julien had revised ambitions of becoming a lecturer and wanted to become a barrister. I could just imagine his tall, lean figure topped by a white wig.

I wandered across the university grounds in the winter sunshine, heading for the library. I no longer ached. I was in a state of total relaxation and contentment. The feeling was so alien to my nature that it startled me.

Would even I look back on this as a golden

time? What a curious thought.

But look out, just when I thought that all was well, remember what happened last time. Stop this. What's wrong with feeling happy?

I had a little moan to one of the lecturers that no one was giving us any guidance on essay writing. He recommended some exponents of the art, and I read them and wallowed in a mass of nit-picking argument over obscure words and phrases couched in what, to me, was boring prose. Depression set in.

What was an essay? That seemed to be a startling and fundamental question to be asking myself. The problem was we were not even given an essay question to answer. Pose your own questions, we were told.

In one essay on Shakespeare's *Coriolanus*, a play I did at A level, I threw in every argument I could muster. The professor ringed the first sentence in which I claimed that Shakespeare filled his hero's dialogue with military metaphors and martial phraseology.

'That should be the sole subject of this essay,' he said. 'You should explore that assertion in detail.'

That was some guidance, but I was humbled after my next effort. Totally baffled by a long obscure poem, I had gathered up different views on the piece as expressed by a number of eminent critics. I set them all out neatly, proving, so I thought, that I had at least done some research.

There was a humbling comment in the margin of the essay when it came back. 'Setting out other people's views on a poem, like a row of dead fish on a slab does not add up to an essay. I want to know what you think about this poem.'

★　★　★

Tanya, bright, bustling and with her braided hair swinging, dumped her large, coloured, canvas shoulder bag on the bench beside me in the lecture hall. 'Hi! How goes it?'

This was typical Tanya, chirpy, in your face and inquisitive. I moved up to make room as she fished out books, note pads and pens.

'Always wanted to ask you,' she said. 'What did you do ... When you worked that is ... ?'

'I was a journalist.'

'Wowee, that's what I fancy doing. You can give me some tips. How did you get into that, then? Come on, give.'

'I don't think you could follow my route.'

'Try me!'

55

'I was going to be a civil engineer on the railway . . . '

'So . . . ?'

'So they found out I was colour-blind.'

'Never!'

'Too true. I would have fastened the red wire to the green wire and crashed all the trains from here to Kings Cross.'

'Never!' said Tanya again. She seized her canvas bag and pointed to one of the coloured patterns. 'What colour's that?'

'Green?' I said hesitantly.

'It's brown! What's that?'

'Sort of beige?'

'It's pink!'

'Told you so.'

'Poor old you.'

'It doesn't hurt much,' I joked, 'but I couldn't become a civil engineer.'

'So you became a colour-blind journalist instead.'

''Fraid so.'

★ ★ ★

The conversation ended abruptly; the lecturer was up on the podium. We were in for yet another lecture on critical theory. Duty had driven me to the lecture hall; I was building up a good head of steam over the gobbledegook surrounding 'critical theory.' Was it going to be more dense thought and problematisation? If so, bring it on!

The guest lecturer was from Cambridge — an extremely tall, spindly, young man in an open neck shirt and jeans; he looked as if he had just escaped from the sixth form. He was introduced as a northerner working in the south, as opposed to our lecturers who were southerners doing missionary work in the north; I conjectured that this was an attempt to make him appear to be one of us.

There was no need for such devices to make him welcome; the young man spoke, and suddenly a searchlight of reason and understanding illuminated the hall. He explained the history of literary criticism, its early forms and the different approaches to its analysis. Incomprehensible phrases that had been thrown at us in earlier lectures now glowed with meaning. This shy young man blew away the obscuring clouds as all the latest 'isms' were put in simple terms. At last I thought I knew what the others were trying to say.

The lecturer's concluding words were, 'Many of the recent authorities on critical theory suffer from a crippling inability to explain themselves, and I find that deeply worrying.'

He sat down and, instead of the desultory clapping that usually greeted the end of a lecture, the massed ranks of students burst into enthusiastic applause. I had not been alone in my ignorance and confusion.

★ ★ ★

We were at a friend's birthday party with everyone chattering around us when I overheard someone ask Meriel, 'Is John enjoying being a student?'

'Having the time of his life,' she said.

And then came another question. 'What's it like having a student in the house?'

Meriel took a deep breath. 'Can be a bit wearing. There's a limit to how much second-hand learning this happy cabbage can take.'

It annoyed me when she called herself that, but I pretended not to hear. Harry, a former university lecturer himself, was part of the group and chipped in, 'It's all very new and exciting for him. Of course he wants to talk about it. You must make allowances.'

'I do,' said Meriel. 'Believe you me, I do.'

Harry, God bless him, got me into a corner later that evening. 'You'll have to watch it, you know. Keep a sense of proportion, dear lad. Keep the home fires burning and all that.'

He was right, but then resentment crept in. Of course I wanted to talk about 'it', because at last I felt I had something to talk about. All my working life I had been a professional listener, politely murmuring, 'how interesting,' at appropriate intervals. It was my job to observe and listen, but unfortunately it had spilled over into my social life; I was always the person who asked the questions that got other people talking on their pet subjects, but now I wanted to hold forth myself. And why not? Because you were probably boring them to death, that was why. Depression followed the resentment. Was my permanent role in life to be a listener?

★   ★   ★

Christmas was approaching. College dinners were being organised and parties arranged. Shu Lin asked me for a list of good eating places in town. I obliged while wondering what I might be unleashing on the local catering establishments. She asked if I would like to join her gang for a night out. I was mildly flattered, but refused, I suspected much to her relief.

★   ★   ★

Meanwhile at home I was badgered into getting my hair cut for the festivities. In my new role as a student I was accused of letting myself go.

'I know your brain's on walkabout most of the time,' said Meriel, 'but I'm not having you looking like some shabby old scruff. Tidy yourself up.' And after the stick came the carrot. 'Besides you look years younger when you've had a decent hair cut.'

* * *

With the end of term approaching it was our last Anglo-Saxon seminar. In eight weeks the lecturer had made a foreign language not only fascinating, but frequently comprehensible. He thanked us for being such an intellectually inspiring group — I bet he said that to all his classes — and as a light-hearted end to the course we translated Anglo-Saxon riddles.

Our early ancestors had a very coarse sense of humour. The riddles always had two answers, the obvious one being extremely rude. Our lecturer posed the first riddle, the innuendo behind which made my eyebrows shoot up.

Without a trace of embarrassment one of the girls piped up, 'The answer to that one is a willie.'

'Shame on you,' said the lecturer when the laughter subsided. 'The proper answer to that one is a key. By the way, does anyone know how an Anglo-Saxon lock works?'

This poor fish rose to the bait. 'I do. There's a reproduction one in the local museum.'

'How does it work?'

Here we go. I am off again, centre stage.

'You have this hole like this and a sort of key thing that you insert like this.'

And here I am demonstrating graphically with my hands and fingers. The lecturer is grinning and the seminar collapses in hysterics. Oh you silly, silly man. How did you fall for that one!

* * *

Christmas decorations went up in the dining halls. Kerry and Sarah both presented me with Christmas cards addressed to John and family. I felt quite touched. Shu Lin told me they had had a great pre-Christmas party. They had not, of course, gone to any of the places on my list — thank goodness, but to an American beef burger bar where, incongruously, all the waiters were Italian.

Shu Lin was eager to supply details. 'We girls got there first, and we told these

61

gorgeous men waiters to chat up the boys. Pretend that they fancied them. Long looks, hands on shoulders. The lot. What a laugh! Were they embarrassed! Showed them what we girls have to put up with!'

I could just imagine. Great party. Glad I missed it.

★　★　★

A rather odd Christmas break was taking place dominated by the *Canterbury Tales*, which had to be explored in detail before the new term started. I knew the stories well, but not in the original Middle English. I spent hours in a slow crawl through the text, verse by verse, with one finger in the glossary at the back of the book. Frustration was building. I was supposed to be studying English, but first there was incomprehensible Anglo-Saxon to negotiate and now Middle English. I never expected to have difficulty in reading my own language.

My head was always in a book and all through the festive season my thoughts were elsewhere.

'You look ghastly,' said Meriel. 'You're doing too much. You're supposed to be on holiday.'

7

Back at 'school'. After a nervous perusal of notice boards and lecture lists, I was at the preliminary meeting for the dreaded Middle English course. The tutor was Mrs. R, a formidable middle-aged lady whose photograph I had seen in the local papers leading rallies and carrying banners proclaiming, 'Reclaim the Night for Women'. There had been a number of assaults on women in the city and the university had a huge girl population. Women were demanding more police action and Mrs. R was leading the campaign. I nervously awaited our meeting.

This was to be my first encounter with a female tutor.

★ ★ ★

It was in my nature to be charming to middle-aged ladies — a legacy of having to give talks to Women's Institutes and luncheon clubs during my working career. My highest accolade in that field had come after talking to a WI group of some twelve members in a wooden pavilion way up in the Yorkshire dales. A very elderly, well-dressed lady had sat in the front row and had watched me intently throughout. When it came time for my cup of tea and biscuit the WI secretary whispered in my ear, 'Congratulations. That was a first.'

'First for what?'

'You kept Lady Smethurst awake. She always falls asleep when we have a speaker.'

Setting that aside, I was well aware that my manner with ladies had its critics. Meriel remonstrated, 'Why is it that within two minutes of you talking to some woman she ends up smiling and laughing? You just can't resist chatting them up can you?'

I was genuinely indignant about such accusations.

'I am not chatting them up. I'm just being friendly and doing my best to be polite and charming. Why not? I've spent my working life talking to people in all walks of life trying to get information out of them and you don't get anything from anybody by being snooty.'

'You know what I mean!'

* * *

I brooded on this rebuke and decided that my lady tutor would have to be approached with some caution. What I regarded as my normal, gentlemanly manner would have to be put on

64

hold in case it was misinterpreted. I could not afford to be accused of 'chatting up' a lady lecturer.

★ ★ ★

Star of our new Middle English group was Tanya, the bouncy, cockney girl whose parents came from Jamaica. Her grin was as cheerful as ever and her dreadlocks still rattled.

'Hi!' she said as she came into the room. 'How's it going?'

Before I could respond Mrs. R breezed in and handed out reading lists, 'Now I want some input from you. Any study ideas?'

Tanya chirps up, 'I don't want to do Chaucer. I am sick to death of bloody Chaucer.'

'We can't do Middle English without doing some Chaucer,' said Mrs. R.

'I've just had him right up to here,' said Tanya wiggling her fingers high above her head and grinning. 'When I was at college that is . . . '

'Then you will have some very authoritative things to say about him in the seminars, won't you?'

Another girl who had been slouching in her chair and staring at the table with glazed eyes started to talk, but without either moving or looking up. The voice seemed to be disembodied and there was momentary confusion as from where it was coming. 'I'd like to study the beginnings of feminism in the early medieval period.'

'We can do that. There are some very fine medieval women writers and characters.' Mrs. R mentioned names and some female characters in the *Canterbury Tales*. At one name she saw a flicker of recognition on my face and to my alarm she pounced. 'You've read that story, John? What did you think of her?'

What did I think of her? I racked my brain. 'As I remember, the woman in that story was a bit of a pain.'

Mrs. R laughed. I was doing it again! But I was now aware that the glazed eyes across the table had come into focus and were staring at me with cold hostility.

'Are you saying that women characters are a pain?'

All eyes were upon me.

'No, just that particular one. I've got a lot of time for the *Wife of Bath* for instance.'

As a suppressed giggle went round the table I realised I should not have said that. There I was, a typical male, picking out the sexy bits.

'Humph!' said the girl with glazed eyes, and to my alarm I realised she was slowly gathering her senses for some devastating riposte.

But before she could strike Mrs. R said briskly, 'Quite so, all sorts of characters, all sorts of themes for us to explore.'

She launched into some of the other literature we would be studying, but my comfortable complacency had been shaken. Was I on the edge of the feminist minefield?

Looking around the group, I saw that the male gender was outnumbered by twelve to three and one of 'ours' was a hippy, wearing an ear-ring and a pink and white Andy Pandy suit.

★   ★   ★

My personal supervisor had invited all his students to his home for drinks. He said Meriel would be more than welcome, but she was doubtful. As a happy cabbage, she insisted that it was not her scene, but then she changed her mind; I was sure it was just curiosity about the sort of company with which I was now mixing.

The large terrace house had a gloomy entrance passage leading to an even gloomier sitting room. Four girl students were perched on a huge Victorian sofa as mute and motionless as a Greek frieze. My supervisor took our coats whispering, 'Hello,' as if he did not want to break the silence. His young wife emerged from the kitchen, handed round drinks and disappeared again. In the gloom I saw Anna sitting in the corner on a high-backed easy chair, her face a picture of amused horror. I took Meriel over and introduced her.

The two were off like a prairie fire, admiring each other's dresses and whispering like conspirators about the lack of party atmosphere. I tried to make conversation with the Greek frieze as our host came and went handing around nibbles and topping up drinks. I decided I had been to livelier funerals.

'Don't you ever take me to a do like that again,' said Meriel, as we drove home. But she had been impressed by Anna. 'Now that girl's got a bit of breeding and intelligence about her. She's the one you keep telling me about, isn't she?'

'Yes.'

'Very attractive girl.'

'Do you think so?'

'Yes I do.' There was a pause. 'Not like those puddings on the sofa.' And after another pause, 'I don't suppose you've been giving them tea and sympathy as well, have you?'

'Certainly not.'

'No, I didn't think you would.'

★　★　★

Kerry still sat beside me in lectures, always complaining gently that she was behind with her essays. Sarah still had her boyfriend in tow; it was revealing to watch the courtship tactics of the young. Sarah was playing it cool: the blonde ice maiden, unsmiling and apparently only half interested in the young man; the occasional flick of the long fair hair, the occasional look. She must have driven that young lad crazy. How different from Anna's frontal assault on the shy Richard.

I marvelled how the young could cope with the pressures of study and all those churning, pulsating hormones. How did they concentrate? They were young that was how. I'm glad I'm not young any more.

And then suddenly there was some excitement for me to contend with; I was going to be in the news! Maggie, one of the feature writers from my old newspaper, wanted to interview me for an article on *Le Troisième Age*. They sent along a photographer and he dashed in full of wisecracks and tales from the office, and in a hurry as newspaper photographers always are. Maggie meanwhile gave a very good impression of being fascinated by every word I uttered. How strange to be at the receiving end of all this journalistic attention.

I remembered Tom, our leading exponent of telephone wheedling. His great skill was to agree fervently with the exponents of both sides of some fierce local row that was hitting the headlines. 'I do so much agree with you,' he would say to each side in turn. 'You are so absolutely right. Their attitude is quite appalling.' And the good folk on the other end of the phone would pour out their woes to the nice young man.

But Tom did have a conscience and often he would put down the phone and mockingly moan for all to hear, 'What a rotten, lying bastard I am!' Whether he was or not, we all admired his skill and he went on to achieve fame and by-lines in London.

But it was Maggie who was sitting in front of me scribbling in her notebook as I talked. 'When do they want all this by?' I asked.

'Tomorrow. They're tying it in with some new Government statistics about older people going back into education.'

Skilfully she kept me talking, took notes, and asked questions, until she, too, rushed off to meet her deadline.

She left me pondering; two people from my past had flitted in and out of my new life and given me a glimpse of what my life used to be. I was impressed by their brisk efficiency and at the same time I felt a twinge of envy. There was a buzz and excitement about their life. I thought I had contentedly entered *le troisième âge*, but there I was looking back nostalgically to *le deuxième âge*.

★ ★ ★

That interview with Maggie disturbed me more than I realised; it triggered a number of work-related dreams. In these dreams I was always at some big event and all the other reporters had got some vital piece of news that I had missed; my deadline was rapidly approaching and I was in a panic. I would tell myself crossly, even while still asleep, that I was not working any more, only to slip straight back into that same fraught dream world. I suspected that it was just my subconscious trying to balance out that twinge of envy of those still at work by reminding me of the everyday realities.

As I rationalised them at dead of night, I remembered Meriel's conversation with our friend Harry who since his own university days had become a Samaritan. He had often regaled us with the troubles of his anonymous telephone clients.

Meriel, a down-to-earth Yorkshire girl, had told him. 'Honestly! Why don't you just tell them to pull themselves together?'

Exactly, why don't I do just that?

8

A symposium was being held with visiting academics and for some reason this was causing a stir among our lecturers. Never having been to a symposium and not really sure of its purpose I attended out of curiosity. But first I took the trouble to look the word up: 'a philosophical or other friendly discussion,' said the Concise Oxford, which added that this could involve 'contributions on one subject from various authors'.

Most of the upper echelons of the English Department were sitting in the front row with eager looks on their faces and there was a fair sprinkling of students in the seats behind them. Onto the rostrum strode a visiting professor of English Literature, a bearded figure in smart casual wear, followed by an Indian gentleman, and then by a severely attractive woman who, we discovered, was an academic celebrity from America.

The professor took the chair with an affected, condescending, nonchalance, which I instantly found irritating. He introduced the subject matter: What is good English literature? Not that again!

Off we went picking apart the meaning of words. 'What is meant by English? Is it work written by English people or does it mean the language? If so, what about Indian English literature, American literature?' said the Indian gentleman.

The American lady entered the fray with terrifying intensity and lucidity. She worried that poor word 'good' to death with the viciousness of a Jack Russell terrier. 'Who said it was good?' she demanded. 'And how was it being judged? From what cultural or social point of view?'

I detected an echo of a previous lecturer's demand to 'problematise' and question the questions.

The Indian gentleman seized his opening and proposed a more culturally-based approach to literature; a lecturer in the body of the hall agreed and said there should be more study of ethnic minority English literature.

Another interposed, 'Yes, but only if it were good and significant and not just because it came from an ethnic minority.'

'And who decides if it were 'good and significant',' said the American lady sharply returning to the fray.

The professor was looking uncomfortable. I suspected the symposium was not following the comfortable paths of learning that he had intended.

The American lady was in full flow again and it was becoming clear she was focussing her attack. She painted a picture of a smart living room in which everyone had been discussing the same literary subject among themselves for years. 'But how did they get into that parlour to join the discussion?' she asked. 'Had only certain types of people been allowed to join in?'

'Would you have been invited in, for instance, if you had been a Black African?'

The professor was stirring in his seat and the American lady eyed him sideways.

Suddenly she posed another much more personal question: 'Why is it that all professors of English literature, wherever you go, all look exactly like our professor here?'

There was a burst of laughter, but also a murmuring undercurrent of disapproval. Our white, upper-class professor looked angry. Was there going to be blood on the senior common room floor after this?

It was all getting rather unpleasant. I could not follow it all, but it seemed to me that this argument over what was good literature was not just shifting the goal posts, it was digging up the whole pitch.

Afterwards, in the corridor outside, I found

the American lady surrounded by chattering admirers, all women. I heard her say to general nods of approval, 'It is good to open out these topics and let in some fresh air.'

Further down the corridor there was a smaller quieter group around the visiting professor of English literature who I suspect was regretting his visit. As I passed I heard a colleague saying to him earnestly, 'I do ask myself if we should be unpacking things in this way in front of the students.'

That, I told myself, was a very sensible opinion.

* * *

I retreated to the library to let my brain slow down and saw that large notices had appeared saying, 'Do not deface books by writing in them'. I knew this disease was spreading, like an attack of measles. I felt sorry for the library staff, but I found the scribbled notes of others in the margins of literary masterpieces strangely satisfying; they were a link with the legions of students who had gone before me. I felt I was not alone; I was one of them in spirit, sharing their incomprehension on one page and their sudden enlightenment on the next. Sometimes they underlined the important passages, quite reprehensible I know, but extremely helpful. Thank you, dear fellow searchers after knowledge; that was exactly the bit I wanted to know!

But then I found a book in which vandalism had reached a new level. Some poor Japanese student had been wrestling with the medieval masterpiece, *Piers Plowman*. I turned a page and every square inch of white margin was covered with vertical columns of minute Japanese calligraphy. It was so neat and perfect it could be displayed as a work of art, but I doubted if the library staff would have seen it in that light. After all the squabbling about what was good English literature, I found those meticulous columns of minute symbols pleasantly soothing; they created a calming sense of order.

Heaven save me! Was I now being brainwashed by oriental mysticism?

★ ★ ★

A winter gale disabled the old apple tree in the garden, the one we used to have as a tree house for the kids; it was leaning drunkenly. It still had its rope ladder leading up to half-a-dozen rotting planks where the 'gang' used to hide and throw apples at passing adults. Meriel said we would have to get someone in to clear it away. I said it might recover. I am back twenty years dreaming about all the fun that tree had given us and I did not want to see it die and be minced up into chipboard. Meriel gave me a very queer look.

Penny visited. The baby had begun to show. Her confidence and independence was a source of pleasure and at the same time a strange selfish sadness. Once she had leaned on us, but no longer. I remembered locking myself in the bathroom and wiping away the tears before we took her to university; how I was full of rousing stories about what fun she would have; those desperate, tearful homesick telephone calls, always late at night. The agonies of worry until the next call and a cheerful voice proclaiming, 'We had a great night out last night!' And now she was married and living miles away.

But there was sometimes a suspicious hint of briskness behind the self-confidence, a briskness, which I thought I understood and in the understanding admired all the more. We knew her too well and she knew us. The secret was not to do anything that could break that fragile emotional armour that we had all put around ourselves in those early days. The armour would grow stronger and inevitably become unnecessary, but then I sensed it could still be thin. I showed her the collapsed tree-house, my thoughts in the past and filled with memories of a noisy, child-filled garden.

'Oh dear,' she said and that was all.

I was given the briefest of looks. It was a look that said, 'Yes, fine, OK, but let's get on with our lives, shall we?' Quite right, too. Don't be such a sentimental old fool. It was all those melancholy poems wailing on about the passage of time and youth that created these maudlin thoughts. Never mind the old tree we had a grandchild on the way!

* * *

My morale was always on a roller-coaster ride at this university. It went down when some lecture topic left me completely baffled, but momentarily it was up. I had my end of term report and Dr P had called me the pillar of his seminar group.

'Who's a clever boy?' said Meriel.

I glowed in the feeling that I must have got something right, but then again with Dr P I was stomping around in familiar territory, the Greek myths and the Old Testament. I had read them all in the past, but now warning bells were ringing. Soon I would be in uncharted, unread, literary waters and I would not have years of pleasure reading to draw upon.

My supervisor handed over my end-of-term report without comment. I was the oldest student ever to pass through the English department and I felt there must have been some comment about my presence. I gently quizzed him. Had there been any feedback from the lecturers? Was I talking too much in seminars? He appeared surprised at my questioning; his other students, I suspected, did not usually invite criticism. The response was an enigmatic smile, 'No, nothing at all.'

We discussed a forthcoming long essay and I sensed a hesitation in his manner. 'About your writing style.' There was an even longer pause as he searched through his mental thesaurus trying to find the right words. 'You do tend to indulge in . . . '

Now what?

'A great deal of persuasive rhetoric.' He appeared pleased with the phrase, for he repeated it. I wondered if this was a good or bad thing.

'Oh dear,' I said, in the hopes of further explanation.

'You have to make sure you have fully examined and understood the text before you attempt to persuade your reader to accept your particular views on it. Always reread the text before you start writing about it. Make sure you really know what it is telling you.'

I brooded on this advice later and realised that he had shrewdly spotted a serious flaw in my whole makeup and also more particularly in my approach to literature. I was far too quick to seize the obvious explanation for any situation and at university had been equally quick at seizing the most obvious meaning of any text. I would then gallop off triumphantly to the word processor and expose the patently obvious to the full blast of my 'persuasive rhetoric'. I was like little Jack Horner pulling one plum out of his pie and considering himself a very good little boy indeed. I was worried. How many 'plums' had lurked undiscovered in all the 'pies' I had already sampled?

As ever I found an excuse: that's what working for newspapers did for you, I told myself, speed-reading a fifty page report and doing a four-hundred-word summary against the clock. I shuddered to think how many nuances of meaning I had missed during my working years. My excuse then had been a good one, too: there was not time to read it again. But I did not have that excuse now. My supervisor had given me some invaluable advice. Slow down. Read it again.

And that got me thinking about something else: *Little Jack Horner*. That nursery rhyme had never made sense to me except perhaps as an admonition not to be a messy eater. But perhaps the nursery rhyme was far more subtle than that. Was it saying do not be a 'one plum' critic, always examine the whole 'pie'?

Is this what they call lateral literary thinking?

Here I go again, staring into space. I never will get the lawn cut.

9

There was a phone call from our son-in-law Steve: Penny had gone into labour.

We awaited a telephone call, which Steve said should be in a couple of hours. Four went by, and I had a gnawing feeling at the pit of my stomach. Meriel was not saying much, but she was fussing around the house tidying up things that did not need tidying.

Another phone call:

'Things are not going quite as expected and we are still waiting.'

'But is she all right?'

'She is being very brave.'

*　*　*

That did it. We went. The motorway blurred and neither of us spoke in the car. Various scenarios were jostling in my mind, all ghastly. The speedometer went above ninety-five miles per hour. Slow down. Why add a road accident to whatever it was we were rushing towards?

I had been reading Ben Jonson and, as I drove with my thoughts swirling, I wished I had not. He had lost his first daughter when she was six months old and then his first son on his seventh birthday, and had poured all his anguish into two short poems. Until that moment I had never thought that poetry could capture such emotions and preserve them with their raw hurt undimmed down the centuries. But even after I had shaken those poems out of my head I started thinking about hospitals

'I hate hospitals,' mother used to say to me every time we visited father. Every time she crossed the threshold it was the same: 'I hate hospitals.' And so did I. Every time I entered one I looked at the people and wondered what traumas they were enduring. I saw them walking anonymously down the corridors or sitting in rows reading outdated magazines in shabby waiting rooms. What were they going through, sitting there waiting and wondering, waiting to be told what, good news or the worst?

★ ★ ★

The same mood overtook me when we arrived. The hospital was old and shabby, with paper notices stuck on doors, which gave me no confidence that an efficient establishment was looking after my daughter.

84

We arrived in the delivery ward and asked about Mrs. Ingham. The nurse was in a chirpy 'how to deal with new grandparents' mode. 'I will let your son-in-law tell you all about it,' she smirked.

Blast the woman! Was Penny all right? I repeated the question more sharply, but she just walked off calling over her shoulder, 'He will tell you all about it.'

All about what, you stupid, stupid bitch!

We went into a room and there was Steve in a surgical gown, glistening with sweat and nursing a baby in his arms. And beside him was an empty bed. The poor lad was unshaven and ashen grey. Our hearts stopped.

'Penny's OK,' he said quickly, seeing the alarm in our faces. 'It had to be a Caesarean. Things went badly wrong and I am very, very angry with this hospital.'

It was a little boy and Meriel took the baby in her arms. 'Oh, you little sod,' she said and burst into tears. Then she touched the baby's cheek and whispered: 'Oh, but you're gorgeous.'

He was the little boy she had lost, the little boy we had both lost.

★　★　★

The other grandparents arrived. This was very odd. This little boy was theirs, too. They wanted to pop champagne. I just wanted to go somewhere quiet and offer up a silent prayer of thanks. I was a granddad!

★ ★ ★

Two honking ducks took off from the campus lake in a frenzied flurry of webbed feet. They came low over the lawns towards the covered walkway, heavy-bodied, and with wings flapping urgently. They were like the RAF bombers I used to watch during the war, struggling to take off in the darkness from the airfield near the town.

On our bicycles, Father and I watched from the country lane and listened to the pulsing roar of the engines. The planes seemed reluctant to leave the ground, clinging to the runway until the last possible moment before they lurched into the night sky. Then they disappeared into the darkness for the long flight to Germany; not all of them came back.

Instinctively we ducked our heads as the birds went over. The sun was shining and the air warm. A duck with a brood of fluff balls in her wake waddled towards the water. Young men and maidens sat on the grass, books laid open unread beside them. Heigh ho! It was spring!

Dr P was in a buoyant mood. He paced up and down the lecture podium in his slightly crumpled, light-weight suit and open-neck shirt and cravat; years ago he must have cut a dashing figure in a Cambridge punt. The students clattered in and he waited until they were settled before fixing them with a mock fierce look.

'Death!' he shouted. In the startled silence that followed he added, 'Has a thousand doors.'

We were into his lecture on John Donne a man who, according to Dr P, rather enjoyed death. For John Donne, death or rather dying was a very busy and creative time. Dr P gave us a dramatic reading of Donne's description of one of his own illnesses commencing with the first 'grudging onset of pain'.

'Marvellous verb that, grudging,' said Dr P smacking his lips. 'And then the physicians were sent for. Not good news that. If the disease didn't get you then the doctors did.'

By now the students were all scribbling and giggling.

'And then pigeons were sent for.'

The good doctor let our curiosity grow. 'Live pigeons were cut in half and clapped upon the body to draw out the humours. Just imagine having half a pigeon clapped on your feet, like feathered slippers.'

The lecture hall was now giggling uncontrollably.

'And another halved pigeon is put on the top of your head, like a feathered bonnet, and in that undignified posture you died, with bits of pigeons at either end.'

There followed a light hearted account of Donne summoning a painter and sculptor to his deathbed so he could pose for his posthumous memorial, 'facing east to show off his good side'.

'The thought of death made him prolific in his writing,' said Dr P. 'That is a useful thought if any of you have writer's block with your essays.'

And then he recounted how Donne had gone off to St Paul's to preach his last sermon. 'Everyone knew he was dying, so everyone turned up to listen. The congregation hung on his words. Definitely the last performance tonight. Roll up! roll up!'

Dr P intoned Donne's stunning words about death, worms and corruption. 'And that's it!' he said, snapping shut his little book. 'I suggest you go out into the sunshine and consider the brevity of life and the joys of dying.'

Hurrah for Dr P! For a whole hour we had

been laughing at death together. The man was an inspiration. I really must reread those Donne poems.

★ ★ ★

My irritation rose with our two lecturers who ran the Turn of the Century course. I had hoped it would be full of HG Wells and Kipling, but I discovered that Kipling was a racist imperialist and one had to wash out one's mouth if one mentioned his name. Instead we are 'into' feminism and anti-imperialism. We were also 'doing' Dracula, which should be fun, but what was this? The deeper meaning of Dracula was apparently the rising threat of female sensuality to a male-dominated world. Never mind Dracula, it was his female vampires that us chaps had to worry about: they and *femme fatales* come from the same nest and threatened the dictatorship of men.

From all the books we were given to read, we were expected to extract themes of female suppression, rape and the struggle by men to maintain their domination over the fair sex. Said our lady lecturer, 'These themes can be clearly seen in the book *King Solomon's Mines.*'

I stirred uneasily. This was one of my

favourite childhood stories.

'This book is about the rape of Africa,' she said, to my growing concern. 'One can see this by studying the journey of the so-called heroes; they travel between the mountains called the Breasts of Sheba . . . '

Yes, I do remember being vaguely uneasy about that as a small boy.

' . . . and then across undulating plains . . . '

Never for one moment had I associated that with a deliciously curved female tum!

' . . . until they came to this hole in the ground: the mine shaft, into which they plunged and plundered.'

Absurd! Ridiculous! Could I believe this? My father had given me a pornographic book to read. We thought it was just a rattling good adventure story. I began looking askance at our lady tutor. A highly-fertile, sexual imagination seemed to be at work here. We were shown slides of threatening *femme fatales* and more female vampires, magnificently bosomed women with wild hair and flowing robes who had men cowering at their feet.

When I reread Ryder Haggard's *She, the one who must be obeyed* I conceded that the lady lecturer might have a point; the book was certainly about attempts at female domination, which, happily from a male point of view, were very firmly crushed. Once again, I felt guilty at my tendency to make 'one plum' snap judgements.

But then my male hostility was aroused once again. One lecture on female vampires ran over time and there were impatient rustlings in the corridor outside. The next lecturer put his head round the door.

'Just another few minutes,' said our lady lecturer sharply.

'You are already ten minutes over your time.'

The girl next to me, an adoring disciple, was incensed. 'Did you see that arrogant male pig,' she hissed at me. 'How sexist can you get?'

Head down, John, say nothing.

Our next book on this course was about yellow wallpaper. Intrigued, I turned the pages. It was all about a woman crawling around the nursery floor going slowly mad and seeing things coming out of the yellow wallpaper. Her husband, naturally, was an arrogant, sexist, controlling male pig who called her 'baby'.

I realised then that I was being pushed out of my comfort zone and I did not like it; and at the same time I was overtaken by a nagging doubt. Had I become so set in my own opinions and attitudes that I automatically rebuffed anything that ran counter to them?

If that were so then what was the point of me being at university? Had I shut the door to anything new and different? Had the age gap finally yawned and become an unbridgeable chasm?

I was alarmed at the thought. This must not be allowed to happen. I must be more open-minded and receptive. For a start, I vowed not to be so hostile towards female vampires with magnificent bosoms.

★ ★ ★

While eating dinner one night Meriel said, 'Would your student friends like to come for a meal one evening?'

Julien, Anna, Richard and Shu Lin were invited. Richard looked embarrassed at the invitation, but only until he revealed that he was vegetarian.

'Tell him he's having fish,' said Meriel.

I picked them all up from university. The girls were smartly dressed and carrying flowers and the boys brought a bottle of wine. It was a lively evening, full of chatter.

Julien was charming, formally thanking Meriel on everyone's behalf: 'Like being back at home again.'

'And a lovely change from Julien's pasta,' said Anna.

Afterwards Meriel said, 'They are a lovely, lovely bunch of kids. It was just like having Penny's friends in the house all over again.'

'I knew you'd like them.'

'But I tell you what,' said Meriel, airing her female intuition, 'that relationship between Anna and Richard won't last. She's far too sophisticated for him.'

* ★ ★

Despite the pleasant social side of my new life the pressure to study was increasing. Two books had to be read in less than a week and half a dozen poems dissected and prepared for seminars . . .

Julien invited me round to his room for tea and we moaned about the work load. The mugs were still stained, but the tea was good and hot. Julien complained that he was not getting on with his supervisor.

'I went in to have a chat about changing some of my courses and she greeted me with, 'I hope this won't take long.' What a thing to say!'

I sympathised. We all seemed to be travelling down a long dark tunnel with no end in sight.

10

Our Turn of the Century Literature course was being examined by seminar presentations, made in pairs. The titles of the 'talks' depressed me. They were all variations on the theme 'feminine voices in *fin-de-siècle* literature'.

At least the presentation by Deborah and me was different: *Play up and Play the Game*, we called it. '*The influence of literature on the Empire builders.*'

During the presentation seminars one could feel the tension in the air. The girls were all wearing dresses and makeup and it was astonishing how attractive most of them looked, having abandoned their ubiquitous jeans and sloppy sweaters. I immediately felt guilty at such shameful sexist thoughts, but wait a minute, why had they bothered? Surely it was an attempt to influence the male examiner? There could be no other reason for all this femininity on display so why was I feeling guilty? They were the ones playing the sex card. As if in confirmation Deborah hissed at me that Rita would do well, because, 'The lecturer fancies her'.

Rita was so nervous her voice was shaking. I felt strangely isolated from all this tension. I really could not get myself worked up into a state over a ten minute talk, perhaps I should. Dared I admit it, I enjoyed this sort of thing. I passed round our illustrated handouts, but there was none of the usual banter, everyone in the room seemed frozen.

'Have you all got your hymn sheets?' I said, fruitlessly trying to brighten the atmosphere, but the world out there was ice-cold, silent and grim.

I started off as brightly as I could and was surprised to see our examiners grinning. I was at it again, playing up to the audience and milking the punch lines. 'Watch it, you are on a time limit.' I speeded up and handed over to Deborah. Then it was back to me. I tore apart Baden Powell's *Scouting for Boys* for its racist undertones — may my old scoutmaster forgive me, but I was learning: I needed the grades and I knew what pleased my judges. Besides, it was my personal conviction that everyone in Victorian times was a racist any way, if by that one meant that they believed white people were superior. Of course they thought themselves superior; poor old Rudyard Kipling was sneered at for expressing the attitudes of the day.

But wait a minute. How about, 'You are a

better man than I am, Gungha Din?' Surely that was not the voice of a racist?

But instantly I heard the counter argument, 'typical hypocritical condescension of the elite'. I was doing a frightening lot of this lately, my brain taking off and disappearing down a branch line.

At least it seemed to be working after a fashion.

Deborah and I wound up our presentation on time and in stony silence. Ah well, that was that. I had survived the Turn of the Century Literature course, becoming slightly more open minded in the process, but with all my male chauvinistic, imperialistic prejudices reasonably intact. Never mind the stirring of feminism, the voluptuous temptations of female vampires and the rampant racism of a shameful British Empire, Alan Quartermain and Kipling's *Soldiers Three* were my heroes still.

★　★　★

That one course, while irritating, had opened up a mental querying about the teaching methods at the university. At times, with the Turn of the Century course I felt I had been told what to find and what to think, and that I had very much resented. On other courses when a student pleaded, 'What does this mean?' the reply was usually, 'What does it mean to you?' Advice might then be given as to where the answer could be found. We were not being taught, we were being helped to discover and decide for ourselves. This, I suppose, was an admirable way of receiving information unsullied by a lecturer's personal views. But while I resented being 'taught' I was becoming a little uneasy about the 'discovery' method. How were we to know that we had discovered what we were supposed to discover? Seminars were the places where it could be revealed that the light had dawned, but often they were confused affairs. Sometimes, I felt that a few gentle hints and clues about what we were supposed to be discovering from a text would have been helpful; the hints could have come with an academic health warning that other interpretations were there to be found.

This debate kept going round and round in my head. This blasted university had got me thinking and questioning and, as they had also insisted, even questioning the questioning.

Fair enough, but would I ever find any answers?

★　★　★

Mike, the tutor for 17th century literature was a man with a vast amount of knowledge, which poured out of him at breakneck speed. His lectures and seminars were sprinkled with references to the many books he had written, commissioned or edited. The man bustled with energy; walking eagerly up and down the lecture room as he talked, up onto the podium one moment and down again the next, a constant excited pacing accompanied by waving arms. Not for him the calm address from the lectern.

He was a much calmer animal at seminars at which Julien was our star performer. A friendly antagonism had developed between lecturer and student, which both seemed to enjoy. Julien liked to question and argue. More and more I could imagine him in wig and gown pleading his case before some High Court judge. In seminars, whenever Mike questioned Julien's comments the student always attempted a comeback. It became a matter of honour to argue. But on one occasion after Julien had explained some interpretation of a book character in great detail there was a disturbingly long silence from the lecturer.

Eventually he said, 'I always seem to be disagreeing with you, Julien, but on this occasion I do believe you are absolutely right.'

There was laughter around the table

'Oh dear,' said Julien dryly. 'That's very worrying. Perhaps I have got it wrong after all.'

★ ★ ★

The family arrived and our ordered life was happily abandoned as a small child became the focus of attention. We were left in charge while the parents escaped to visit friends. We changed nappies, played games, and exhausted ourselves. My eyes watered, staring through the crack of the door to make sure he was still breathing in his cot. Then just as suddenly the family went back home and there was a sudden silence, an emptiness. Why did they have to live so far away? Meriel started spring cleaning and I cranked up the computer and wrestled with the problems of courtly love, as revealed in *Troilus and Cressida*.

A week later Penny was on the phone: she was down with flu, and James was acting up. With her husband in America for almost a week she desperately needed help. Meriel was immediately looking up train timetables. 'If it wasn't for that damn university of yours we could both go down there now and help her. You're supposed to be retired. Why are we up here when she needs us down there?'

Meriel travelled south by train and became a mum again. I stopped at home guiltily attending lectures, reading books in a very silent house and thinking that I, too, should be down there in support. But I was not.

Apart from compulsory seminars I had two long essays to write, but the deadline was two months away; this gave me no sense of urgency to get them done. I remembered what an old Fleet Street journalist once told me, 'When you've worked under the lash you miss the 'incentive' when it's not there.' How true. So I brought the deadlines forward, those essays would be done before Meriel returned. That way I might have some free time for a normal home life when she came back

* * *

'Hello, John,' said the lady in the English Department Office.

John, she called me John? I must have crossed some social line of acceptance and I felt strangely happy and content. This university was a friendly place and I felt part of it and that it had given me a worthwhile purpose in life.

I handed in my two long essays and my contentment melted in a cloud of doubts.

What if I had gone off completely on the wrong track? What if I had used my 'persuasive rhetoric' on yet another fruitless journey up a gum tree? What 'plums' had I left undiscovered in little Jack Horner's Christmas pie? Too late now.

In the calm of the library Julien hurried in with an air of ill-suppressed panic. 'How well do you know Anthony and Cleopatra?'

I sensed a facetious reply would not be welcome.

'I'm trying to verify a quote and it's a bit important 'cos it's the title of my essay.'

'When is it due in?' I asked, knowing that he had had months to complete it.

'In an hour.'

He disappeared down the corridors of books and a few minutes later he reappeared waving a thumb in the air as he hurried off.

★ ★ ★

I wandered across parts of the campus, which were new to me, trying to find the lair of my new tutor; always an anxious moment encountering someone who was going to dominate and colour my life for the next few months. He had a long, lean aesthetic face and the quiet manner of a learned monk, but he was full of encouraging remarks like, 'That is a very good point' and 'Yes, that is an important question.' Perhaps all would be well, but he had an aura of academic intensity about him that made me nervous and I doubted if much laughter had penetrated his cloister.

When I attended the first lecture of the new term, the lovebirds Richard and Anna were sitting at opposite ends of the room. They usually sat within chatting distance of me so there was immediately a problem in social relations, where should I sit? As Richard was the closest I dumped my books and papers near him, but I was well aware that Anna was staring from a distance.

'Problems?' I asked.

'We've had a tiff, she's a bit . . . ' And he stopped, sensing watching eyes, and said no more.

'Women usually are,' I said jokingly and he half laughed.

After the lecture Anna was hovering at the end of the crowded corridor talking to some girls, but glancing in our direction.

'For goodness sake,' I whispered to Richard. 'Go and talk to her.' And I turned and walked away, wondering uneasily if I should have even suggested that. I could hear Meriel's voice complaining: 'you're getting involved.'

Later that day I saw them walking across the campus, crab-like, with their arms around each other and she was nibbling his ear. But having avoided one 'situation' I immediately found myself on the fringe of another. In the snack bar Deborah, a seminar colleague from last year, brought a cup of tea and sat unbidden at my table. This was a surprise. She was an older student, streetwise and hard-eyed in her Doc Martin boots and leather jacket; she was the only girl student I had met who looked you straight in the eyes when she talked.

'Wondering what I'm going to do when all this is over,' she said without preamble.

'What do you want to do?'

'I don't want to go back to nursing, that's for sure.'

I let the conversation hang there.

'I was going to get married but that's out now.'

I muttered something noncommittal. Her eyes bore into mine and there was a pause during which both of us were obviously assessing and wondering. Then she made the decision and the shutters came down. Abruptly she switched the conversation to the course she was on. At that point, if she had been my daughter I would have said, 'Come on, what's the matter? Tell me?' But I did not.

She wanted to talk, but, I suspected, getting no encouragement, the moment passed. I felt guilty and annoyed with myself, but then I had been warned. 'Don't get involved.'

And then there was Melissa, a redhead endowed with all the brisk commonsense of a head girl from an excellent school. She was a friend of Anna's and as such I had been accepted by her as a fellow conspirator in the weekly tutorial skirmishes with our new monkish lecturer. I had learned that he was one of the most highly qualified members of staff with degrees from Cambridge and Yale as well as being on regular call to lecture in Japan. I sincerely felt that such knowledge and teaching talent was cruelly wasted on someone like me who knew nothing about his world of Pope and Dryden.

I was grateful for an ally, because I was struggling. We were joined in the group by Gareth, a round-faced studious lad who started sparkling about Pope and making comparisons across whole centuries of literature. He swapped quotations with the lecturer whose eyes shone like those of a venerable abbot suddenly discovering that at last a genius had appeared amongst the latest oafish intake of novices. My eyes widened in dismay while Melissa stifled a grin. Afterwards she said, 'I should have warned you about Gareth. That boy is seriously clever and I do mean seriously. Starred First, no problem.'

I felt depressed. I was not going to be the pillar of this particular seminar group, in fact I would be lucky and grateful just to survive.

11

Another course started called Patterns of Story. I had read somewhere that there were only five basic plots in the whole of literature. If I learned those five stories and recycled them I felt certain a stream of best sellers and untold wealth would assuredly follow. Judging by the course's popularity most of the English students had the same idea. Oh what simple fools we mortals be! We wallowed in a complex morass, which seemed to take in the whole of human nature, psychology and philosophy, but without, as far as I could see, a clear cut plot coming into sight.

Our first task was to link the Theban plays — Oedipus killing his dad and being over friendly with his mum — with the Book of Job in the Bible. I consulted our vicar for advice: The Book of Job explored the problem of why innocents suffer. If God is benevolent, why did He let nasty things happen to the godly? The Book's conclusion was that by suffering we obtained humility and self knowledge.

Our lecturer, a lady with wild hair and long woolly skirts, curled up her nose when I expounded this theory. 'That is the Christian response. What about all the other responses to the question?'

The talk went round and round and I could see confusion growing.

'Surely,' she said, 'the answer to the question is obvious: it is a hippopotamus.'

Understanding slowly dawned, but only days later. If the question really was, 'Why do bad things happen to good people?' then perhaps a hippopotamus was a very good answer: in other words, there was no answer. But that had not prevented numerous attempts down the ages to find one.

I had very nearly not grasped any of this and my internal debate on teaching methods surfaced with a vengeance. A few sentences chalked up on the blackboard would have explained this first 'pattern of story' very easily without dragging a hippopotamus squealing into the room.

But then that still small voice chipped in again: Can't you see? The system works; you discovered that meaning for yourself. Now you will remember it.

I tried not to be a doubting Thomas, but the other 'patterns of story' passed me by in an incomprehensible haze. I should have had the courage to demand explanations, but I did not. My nerve failed me. Having deciphered one 'pattern of story' I thought I should have deciphered the others. And as there were no questions from the other students I concluded that I was the only dunce. Yet I could not help feeling somewhat aggrieved that something probably quite important had been trailed across my path and I had completely failed to understand it. And I never did discover the five basic plots of literature.

★ ★ ★

The 18th century seminar group gathered in the corridor and Anna joined us. She and Melissa had their heads together in deep conversation and I saw that Anna was close to tears. Now what? Not more boyfriend trouble!

In the seminar it was starkly noticeable that Anna had withdrawn into cold, tight-lipped silence. She pointedly said nothing through-out the whole session. With the brilliant Gareth missing and the other students saying little the silences grew longer and longer. In any case, we were all overawed by our tutor who was meticulous and 'thinking' in all his utterances. Every comment from a student was followed by a lengthy pause, and I could almost see an analytical brain weighing and judging every word before he formulated a reply.

I felt almost as embarrassed as the tutor by the silences and I ran out of the questions that I always jotted down for discussion. He looked long and hard at me and I sensed an appeal for help. I conjured up something to say, but it sounded horribly trite when I put it into words.

The seminar staggered on. Suddenly, after a particularly long silence, he lost patience and told us to open our books at a certain page. 'Anna,' he said, startling her into attention. 'You take the female character there and John, you take the male.'

We had to act out a quarrelsome exchange between two lovers in a restoration comedy. Anna perked up immediately at the chance to perform and it was fun for me, too, as we exchanged insults and witticisms across the table. The mood brightened considerably. Our clever old tutor had saved the day.

★   ★   ★

Afterwards, I adjourned to the coffee bar and Anna and Melissa joined me rather purposefully, Melissa surreptitiously raising her eyebrows at me and inclining her head towards Anna.

'Something the matter?' I asked.

Oh foolish man. Why do you invite trouble?

'That man . . . ' meaning the lecturer, ' . . . is ignoring me!' cried Anna. 'He just doesn't like me. It's because I'm foreign. He knows I can't express myself properly in English.'

Both Melissa and I nearly choked over our coffee. Sensible, head girl Melissa laid into Anna and I nodded my head in support.

'It's because I am foreign. I know it is,' wailed Anna.

'Nonsense,' I said as Melissa and I set about persuading her that the academic staff was not suffering from xenophobia. 'And he's not ignoring you. He picked you out to do that acting bit, didn't he? And you were very good at it, too.'

Anna sniffed and dabbed her eyes.

★ ★ ★

'You're doing it again,' said Meriel, when I regaled her with the story over dinner: 'You're getting involved.'

'Oh no I'm not.'

'Oh yes you are. Let them get on with it. They don't need you interfering!'

★ ★ ★

I was reading the library copy of Joseph Adams and suddenly found myself in the middle of a contemporary feminist debate. The book-defacing plague had spread. A passage in the book mocked a lady for misusing words and this had been side-scored with a comment in pencil: 'Dig at uneducated women who cannot use words properly.'

To which someone else had added: 'You are paranoid. It is called humour, but you femmies have never heard of that.'

And later: 'Another dig at women!'

To which the male critic had added: 'It is boring having someone as thick as you scribbling all over a marvellous book.'

★   ★   ★

Sitting in a lecture, trying to concentrate, and having nothing better to do, I minutely examined the back of my hand. It was covered with small, brown, mole-like markings, all quite natural, but they reminded me of something and I suddenly remembered what.

Good grief, what an appalling thought: My father's hands looked like that the very last time I saw him lying there.

I concluded that I was reading far too much Greek tragedy and far too much poetry harping on about death. Are we never going to study anything cheerful? I jocularly complained to my supervisor, 'Poets are a miserable lot. It's all unrequited love or death — no laughs anywhere.'

'Oh I don't know,' his eyes roved the book shelves behind me, but no mirthful volume was produced.

★ ★ ★

When I got back home I was in rebellious mood so I found a P.G. Wodehouse and had a good giggle at Bertie Wooster. With spirits uplifted I felt fresh to face the world again. And then I wondered: had I discovered a serious gap in the university's English literature curriculum? Where was the laughter, where was the humour? Down the ages people had always enjoyed a good giggle, even the Greeks and Romans enjoyed their comedies. Why were we not studying the history of humour or was not that a serious enough topic?

And was not the ability to make people laugh just as important as the ability to make them cry? And was it not more difficult? The subjects and occasions that caused tears were universal throughout time and different societies, but what created laughter was infinitely more complex, was it not?

I was off again. The poor old brain flying away at a tangent. I had enough to study without adding to the work-load.

★ ★ ★

At home I resisted the temptation to share my exciting new thoughts on humour with Meriel. I really tried to keep the university out of everyday conversation, but my world was narrowing and the pace was hotting up. I had to read two 18th century plays by Wednesday, a novel for a seminar discussion by Monday and then James Joyce's *Ulysses* — which by some obscure 'pattern of story', that I never discovered, was linked with Hamlet.

This is fun? Even I cannot enjoy books read at this speed, particularly *Ulysses*. Does anyone enjoy *Ulysses*? Does anyone ever finish reading *Ulysses*?

12

Notices for Christmas get-togethers went up on the notice boards and parties were being organised. For the first time in forty years we were not having Christmas at home. We were at Penny's, playing with young James and watching someone else doing the cooking. But the festive season always makes me maudlin. One became trapped into one's own little world with too much time to think about the milestones of 'the journey' whizzing past the 'window' at ever increasing speed.

For goodness sake cheer up, and enjoy the sight of your grandchild tearing open his presents.

But after that, what: the cold, dark journey through New Year to a distant spring?

Literature gave plenty of advice on this maudlin subject. 'Tend your garden,' said Voltaire, which, I suppose when translated into my own world, meant get back to your books until the lawn needs cutting.

★   ★   ★

And soon, so soon, there we were again, back at college tramping the familiar corridors, seeing familiar faces lighting up in greeting. It was good to be back.

I saw my supervisor for my end of last term's report and, oh dear, he looked slightly embarrassed.

'I don't think your tutor realises that we have to show these to you.'

That sounded ominous.

The verdict has come from the monk and I had not been looking forward to this. The English literature of the 18th century had washed over me in a confusing deluge and I had drowned in it, clutching at fragments of passing learning as I sank.

''He writes pleasant journalistic essays, which I suspect differ little from his writing for his old newspaper,'' said my tutor.

Oh yes! I knew sufficient about academics to realise that the word 'journalistic' was a term of abuse.

''He asks naive questions and I doubt if he has learned a great deal from the answers.''

This from a man whose seminars I had tried to keep going with admittedly desperate off-the-cuff questions!

Then came the comment, ''However, a lively contributor to seminars and one who could be relied upon to prevent them from falling into apathy for which I was personally grateful.''

I revised my opinion of my tutor.

'I think that's fair comment,' I said. My supervisor, bless his heart, looked relieved. He had probably been worried about how I would react.

Then the usual thoughtful silence developed. 'You have the Professor for your next course,' he said at last. His eyes met mine and hesitated. 'You'll find that interesting.'

What did he mean by that?

'Any problems?' he asked.

I shook my head.

'Nothing come back to you about me?' I asked.

Again we went through this little ritual. If my incongruous presence had caused amusement or comment in the Senior Common Room my supervisor was not telling.

'So, into another term,' I said chirpily.

'And the best of luck,' my supervisor had never wished me that before.

A tap on the door announced another student had arrived to receive her report. I gathered up my books and departed for the library wondering why I needed luck for this particular term.

★　★　★

The library had become my favourite place on campus. It was like stepping inside a vast, benign brain, quietly ticking away, friendly and calm, waiting to be consulted, wanting to help. Every time I entered I had a warm feeling that I was starting out on another pleasurable journey of discovery. I would head for a computer terminal and extract my list of needs from the brief case. The computer would buzz quietly and up would come the reference numbers I wanted. Were they in? Yes, said the computer, and then there was the search along the silent shelves.

One irritating problem: why was the book I wanted always at floor level or near the ceiling? I decided that dignity did not matter any more. I squatted on the floor like everyone else to access the bottom shelves and I hoped no one would hear my gasps and creaking bones as I went down. It was worse trying to get up. I dreaded the thought of having to call for help and having someone haul me up onto my feet.

The books on the top shelves were easier to get to; I could stand on one of those wheeled-step devices. Perched up there I must have looked like a hippopotamus, yes that hippopotamus again, but this time balanced on a plant pot.

When my book choices had been made the ladies at the check-out, who knew me well by now, always gave me a cheery smile as they stamped my books. It was the same with the security men who made sure that the university's property was not leaving home illegally. As they checked the date stamps on the heap of tomes in my brief case there was always some comment, 'Nice bit of light reading for you there then. Keep you out of mischief.'

Mischief! When had I got time for mischief?

* * *

We lounged against the wall in the corridor outside the office of the Professor of English, coats and bags dumped all over the floor in untidy heaps. Strange how quickly I had regressed and adopted the habits of the young. This was the lair of the great man himself. Every one was nervous, sizing each other up and clutching their files and books.

The door was flung open and there he was, with his long grey hair standing erect, as if in shock from the turmoil of brain activity churning beneath. Patches of white shirt peeped through the holes in the elbows of his long, woolly pully. His dark eyes darted around the waiting group, but there was not a flicker of surprise that someone even older than himself was waiting there among the youngsters.

'In!' he waved his arms as if rounding up a pack of reluctant hounds.

We sat in a circle of chairs, while he bustled around the room consulting pieces of paper and answering telephone calls. Eventually he collapsed into an armchair amongst us and those piercing eyes fixed themselves on each one of us in turn.

'Right! What do we want to study?'

There was a stupefied silence.

'Come on, you must have some ideas. You! What do you want to do?'

He jabbed a finger at one of the girls and crashed back into his armchair with head cocked on one side eager to listen. The girl turned bright red and muttered something about Shakespearian comedies.

'Right! You!'

The finger jabbed towards another of us cowering wretches. I am vividly reminded of Gagool, the 'smeller out of evil' in that pornographic book, *King Solomon's Mines*. Then he grinned like a naughty schoolboy. 'Sorry. Dreadful to pounce on you like that. But I want your input. Right, let's write this down.'

A term of course work slowly materialised. It was cleverly done giving the impression that we had created it all ourselves.

'First seminar next week. Read these

poems and be prepared to talk about them.'

We dutifully wrote them down, but as he went on slowly adding to the list our unease became palpable. He mentioned one particularly long poem and this was greeted by groans. I was startled. Previous groups I had joined would never have dared react in such a way, but then I realised that these students were predominantly third years, slightly older, and as a result their self confidence was a little more aggressive.

The Professor pretended to look startled. 'You are here to study, are you not? You are all fulltime students.'

The young lady next to me crossed her long, black nylon-clad legs and said coolly, 'But it's important we have some sort of social life as well.'

The group giggled. My eyes widened and I think my jaw must have dropped just a little. The professor saw the look on my face and for the briefest of moments I sensed a meeting of minds.

'Well now,' he said, completely unperturbed. 'Do try and spare us a few hours from your busy social lives if you possibly can. I'm sure you will find it worthwhile.'

We were dismissed. It was clearly going to be an interesting seminar group.

I left the Professor's lair with a daunting

workload in my note book, and a strangely disturbed feeling that I found difficult to understand at first. I concluded that I would very much like to impress this man, but I seriously doubted if I could.

⋆ ⋆ ⋆

The courses were now coming thick and fast and I understood why my supervisor had wished me good luck. I would need it. I was surprised that we were not taking Shakespeare as a course in itself; he was being studied alongside his contemporaries of whom there were quite a few. I got the impression that some of our lecturers were bored to death with Shakespeare. There was a hint of weariness at the very mention of his name. Not *Coriolanus* again!

My impressions were confirmed by a famous visiting lecturer, hailed in advance as *the* authority on the bard. The hall was full, and all our tutors were chattering in the front row. 'I asked Charles what he wanted me to talk about today and his reply was, 'Anything but Shakespeare.' So I'm going to talk about Marlowe,' said our visitor.

There was happy laughter from the front row.

'You might be bored with Shakespeare, my dears, but what about me? And I'm the student here, not you.'

★ ★ ★

The Professor was piling on the pressure, opening up unexpected avenues for study, always questioning and probing everything. Having delved into what I thought were the depths of one of the poems, I rambled on about humanism.

'Yes, yes,' he said, 'but there's more to it than that, surely. What else?'

What else? I had barely understood that bit, never mind considered what else! With the Professor any poorly thought out or weakly expressed criticism was left shredded and bleeding on the floor. But while he growled, he did not bite. Victims of his deft dissections were not left wriggling on the hook for long: a grin, a joke and he released them and chased off after some other deeply buried interpretation. In this man's presence everything seemed to slip into a higher gear and the poor old brain had to be in overdrive just to survive.

I bumped into Dr P in the corridor and he stopped to chat. How was I getting on? What course was I doing? I mentioned that I was with the Professor and he laughed. 'Surviving?' he asked.

'I'm not sure,' I said.

★　★　★

My first essay for the Professor took ages. I toned down my journalistic style and polished the words nervously. My essay was returned with neat comments in pencil in the margins: 'OK, you understand what the poem means, but a poem is more than a thought. What is the verse saying?'

The verse? What did he mean, the verse? With all my essays for him I lay awake at night, questioning, being assailed by doubts.

Did the verse really add meaning beyond the meaning of the words? Round and round it all went. No longer did I feel confident that I had grasped all of a poem's meaning and could dash off an easy essay. Was the over-simplistic logic of old age exposing even to me the shallowness of my critical faculties?

I realised with a jolt that I was back with little Jack Horner. Not only was I now examining every plum and crumb in the Christmas pie, but I was even turning over the plate and looking for the maker's name. Nothing seemed certain any more, no idea, no conclusion was for certain; at times I felt that I was knocking the bricks out from under my feet.

There was just too much to question and think about.

13

Meriel had been watching the mounting pressure with growing alarm.

'How long is this going on for?' she demanded. 'You're doing too much.'

After some debate I responded to her concern by booking myself into the Well Persons Clinic at the doctor's. There had been some disturbing reminders of mortality lately. I played tennis once a week and we had just lost Tony. 'Just lost' was a euphemism; he had just died. He was younger than me and I comforted myself by saying that he was distinctly tubby. After a particularly lively game of tennis he had collapsed and died from a heart attack. He and his wife lived for tennis and everyone was stunned. There was a huge turn-out for his funeral and a week later we, the survivors, were back on court playing tennis a little less energetically than usual. I was partnering Derek.

'What are all these grey bits mixed up with the red shale?' I asked.

Derek looked around nervously. 'Ashes. It was his last request.'

Meriel was appalled, and I pondered all of

this as the doctor took my blood pressure and announced that it was dangerously high.

'Are you feeling under any strain at present?' he asked.

'I am doing this university course.'

I was prescribed some pills.

'And take as much physical exercise as you can without overdoing it, of course.'

Thank you very much! And end up scattered all over a tennis court!

★ ★ ★

When I got back home I checked through my workload for the week, and gave myself a stern talking to about priorities and time allocation. I flicked over the diary pages to find the end of term. Was it really that far away!

I continued my self-lecture. Did I really think I could swan through a university degree course at my age and not put myself under pressure?

★ ★ ★

Meriel and I were invited out to dinner. The formal invitation came from Julien. We arrived outside the three storey, old, terrace house and parked the car among the old bangers littering the street. The tiny, front garden was filled with abandoned bicycles. Julien opened the front door. He had said the evening was to be formal and it was: he was wearing a tie.

Anna, Shu Lin and Deborah were waiting for us in the front room, which appeared to have been rapidly tidied up for our coming. I noticed newspapers, magazines and books stacked in neat piles behind the sofa; from upstairs came chattering, laughter and music. We talked to the girls while Julien busied himself elsewhere, we presumed, in the kitchen.

Eventually his head appeared around the door and the announcement came, 'Dinner is served.'

'God save us all,' sighed Anna. 'He's a lousy cook!'

The dining room was a small space half under the stairs and half in the passage, but furnished with a table and chairs on which were flowers and lit candles.

'Sorry no wine glasses,' said Julien pouring wine into tumblers. 'And I hope you like pasta.'

'Only thing he can cook,' said Anna in a stage whisper as a huge basinful appeared from the kitchen. But it was good pasta and the denigration of the cook was gentle and good-natured.

The meal was great fun, but frequently interrupted. Someone clattered down the stairs above our heads, apologising profusely, and pushed past to get something from the kitchen. Then the telephone rang in the hall and a girl rushed downstairs to answer it.

'Oh it's you,' she said, and our dinner conversation stopped in its tracks; she was only a few feet away from the dinner party. Julien eyed her severely. 'Can't talk now,' said the girl. 'I'll ring you back.'

She ran back upstairs calling, 'Sorry' to the dinner party half hidden under the stairs.

Both Meriel and I were concerned that we were upsetting the happy routine of the student 'digs.'

Julien watched the girl go with a stern look on his face. 'I did warn everyone we were having guests tonight.'

★ ★ ★

I was impressed; I could definitely see that boy in wig and gown; he had the air, the manner, the authority. Meriel was impressed, too.

'They're sweet,' she said to me afterwards 'all of them. Trying so hard to be grown up, but you would think the girls would have contributed something towards the cooking side of things. Not leaving it all to Julien.'

'I'm glad you didn't say that out loud,' I said. 'You would have got a lecture on sexist-stereotyping.'

'Don't you start using your big words on me.'

* * *

Our peripatetic lecturer Mike extended his lectures to two hours, but the sessions were still packed to the doors. The attraction was the videos, which showed different actors at work on the chosen excerpts. Mike always started with what he considered to be the worst performance, mockingly conducting the mechanical word rhythms of one actor, and rolling his eyes in distress as another threw away key phrases.

It was fascinating stuff. We were certainly learning the nuances that a piece could be given and we could also see the depth and skill of Shakespeare's writing and how it could be interpreted in many ways. If I did not learn about Shakespeare from these lectures then I never would.

And had I not complained earlier about not 'doing' Shakespeare separately? Wrong again.

Doubling the length of his lectures did not slow Mike down for a moment. He still stalked the lecture hall, up and down, on and off the podium, a non stop word machine, talking, talking, talking.

★ ★ ★

At last! Oh blessed relief! The spring holidays were upon us. And this time there would be no more pretentious reading of learned books on the beach. My poor brain needed a real rest. I forgot English literature and we went off on a package trip to Rome.

'Would we like to meet the Pope,' asked our courier?

'Why not,' we replied.

A few thousand others had the same idea and St Peter's Square was one vast coach park.

The courier would not let us out of our transport until she had made an announcement. 'You can't get in to see the Pope as tourists so you are all pilgrims for the day. You are the official representatives of St. Margaret's Church in Clitheroe.'

An ill-concealed giggle escaped from the 'pilgrims', but then there was a sense of unease. Those Swiss Guards patrolling outside looked huge. Should we be sneaking into a Papal audience under false pretences?

'Don't worry,' said the courier, 'There isn't

a St. Margaret's Church in Clitheroe.'

My academically-sharpened critical factors failed to see how this resolved the moral issue.

'This is just a device to get tourists in. It happens all the time. And another thing, your presence as pilgrims will be announced from the stage and the Holy Father will acknowledge you. So if you could all stand when your church is mentioned, and if you could all wave . . . Remember, St. Margaret's Church, Clitheroe.'

The Holy Father and I waved to each other across a vast and crowded room. I felt terribly guilty deceiving such a nice old gentleman. Even back home again I kept away from my books and I arranged to meet Stacey, an old journalistic colleague, for coffee. In retirement we used to meet regularly to sort out the world's problems and moan about the deterioration in journalistic standards. University had broken the pattern, but a telephone call re-established the link. For more than forty years we had worked in friendly rivalry on different newspapers as observers and commentators and we had shared all the 'important happenings' in our own little part of the world. There was always much to share and reminisce about.

We met for coffee in a country hotel just

131

outside town expecting a quiet chat, but as we walked into the lounge we had a shock. There they were in all their belligerent glory: the national newspaper gang, the media en masse, the wolves who descended on 'our town' whenever something 'big' broke.

They knew us and we knew them and we were greeted with much joviality and comments about grey old men at leisure. We were both completely out of touch with breaking news, so what had brought them scurrying north? We quickly discovered that there had been a roof collapse in a nearby coal pit and the wolves had gathered smelling blood. The hotel had become their temporary headquarters; lap-tops, cameras and fax machines were plugged into every available power point; and glasses of beer and trays of coffee littered the floor and tables.

We soon gathered that the incident had turned out to be something of a damp squib: no deaths and only very minor injuries. Hearing their complaints I was reminded of the old Stanley Holloway monologue about a trip to Blackpool: 'no shipwrecks and no people drowned, in fact, nothing to laugh at at all.'

Stacey and I retreated into a corner as silence descended, but for the tapping of keys.

'Anyone know who raised the alarm?' asked the man from the Press Association.

'Got a good quote on that,' said the Daily Mail riffling through his notebook. Suddenly he had the room's full attention. 'Yeah, here it is.' Pens were raised as the Daily Mail reporter assumed a very posh voice, 'Quote: 'I say Charlie, old chap, what was that dreadful noise?' Unquote.'

He was greeted with a chorus of, 'Prat!'

The keys start tapping again.

'Where's Dan?' the Northern Echo asked. 'I thought he was the Sun's mining expert. He's good on mine background stuff. He should be out on this one.'

'Never goes out these days,' said The Guardian. 'That's why they call him the lighthouse.'

This was greeted by groans.

'Do you mind?' complained The Times. 'Some people are trying to write here.'

Stacey was laughing quietly and shaking his head, 'That's the only thing I miss. All the banter. Do you remember that press conference after that big union meeting on the dock strike? Chairman told us all pompous like, 'We have been discussing world peace.' And then silence, nothing, so up pops the chap from the Telegraph and asks, 'Can we assume you're in favour of it?''

'Those were the days,' I said. 'But just look at all this hi-tech kit. I remember when we just had typewriters and copy girls.'

'I remember quill pens,' said Stacey.

We watched in something approaching awe. What was happening in front of us was what both of us had once done for a living, but now just the sight of the equipment being used unnerved us.

'You've got to hang onto one thing,' Stacey had a touch of defiance in his voice. 'All that kit is bloody useless until someone gives it some words to play with. It can't write by itself. Without the reporter all that kit is useless junk.'

I nodded in agreement, but as I took in all the flickering laptop screens and the bowed heads I was not reassured. 'Still frightening. There was something reassuring and solid about dictating a story down a telephone to a real live copy girl.'

'Too right.'

We drank our coffee, grinned at the wisecracks, and took our leave. Thank you lads, but no thanks. It's a different world out there and it's a young man's game now.

134

14

Back on campus exams were approaching. After the carefree years, life was becoming very serious indeed. For the students in my year life-deciding options and careers were in the balance yet again. I sensed the growing tension and felt sorry for them. It had started with O levels, then A levels and now it was all building up all over again.

But no career prospects were at stake for me. My working life was over, so what did it matter? And yet somehow it did matter. It mattered a great deal.

'Going to get a First are we?' asked Marion. Her family and ours had holidayed together for years. She had been a teacher and had been a little guarded about my bold excursion into her academic world.

'No chance,' I said. 'My head hit its academic ceiling long ago.'

'What then?'

'No idea,' I said outwardly cheerful, but inwardly praying, 'Please do not let it be a Third.'

★ ★ ★

I had two courses, which could not be further apart in time and language: 20th century American Literature and Racine and Molière — in French. And it was him again — the Professor. I had a terrible fear of showing myself up with my schoolboy French. I swotted through the French plays with a crib in my hand, spending huge amounts of time just understanding the words never mind forming any deep critical opinions.

And then there was American literature taught by a friendly young lecturer in jeans and open neck shirt, with a habit of scratching his armpits when in oratorical flow. But he was a nice chap. So when I was not wallowing in high French drama I wrestled with modern American literature such as the enigmatic short poem, *The Red Wheel Barrow*.

In a tutorial group we were asked for comment. My hackles rose once again. 'What does it mean?'

And back came the usual reply, 'What does it mean to you?'

'Nothing, but as it's in this anthology and we're studying it I suppose it must mean something. I would love to be let in on the secret.'

But as usual I never got a satisfactory answer and we passed on to other things.

My irritation level was rising once again. My cynical journalist nature had still not been completely subdued.

On this occasion I wanted something I could read without a dictionary and something I could understand. University had also not completely killed off the journalistic arrogance, which insisted that if I could not understand something after careful reading then the fault lay not with me, but with the author: it was his job to communicate and clearly he had failed. Besides which, I had an inbuilt suspicion of things that appeared deliberately obscure. And my simplistic mind was also finding other minor irritations.

Take Henry James. Had the man never heard of a full stop? And what about this? 'Outside, he lit, in the street, a cigarette.'

Was this style? Was this high prose?

That disturbing, nagging unease was surfacing again from the depths of my mind. Yet again, was this just the reaction of an old man manning the mental barriers he had set up against something irritatingly new? What about my resolution to be more open-minded?

Oh dear, there I was thinking about thinking again.

In the American seminars our jean-clad

lecturer calmly faced hostility among his students about some of the literature he asked us to read. In one book *The Naked Lunch*, I had never seen so many obscenities crammed onto one page. It was too much for one of the girls. When asked for her opinion she tossed the book into the middle of the table and said dramatically, 'It's a load of crap!'

The young lecturer was not at all put out. 'That's certainly one point of view. But perhaps you could expand on that, just a little?'

A heated discussion followed into which I got drawn. I suggested that all this rude gibberish pretended to be the ravings of someone high on drugs. How was he still able to form sentences and maintain good grammar? The lecturer mused over that comment and said he had never heard the book interpreted in that way before. For a fleeting moment I thought I had come up with something brilliantly new; then the subtle ambiguity of his comment dawned on me; it was far more likely that my idea was new simply because it was ridiculous.

Nothing emerged from the debate, which, in my opinion, contradicted the girl's initial assessment. But, as usual, I had doubts. This was, after all, a famous book, a best-selling classic. So once again I had probably missed the whole point.

Open your mind to new things, young sir, or you are going to spend the rest of your time here walking past closed doors.

★ ★ ★

A heat wave hit. My walks across the campus slowed to a meander. The chestnut spires were out and those fluff-ball goslings were waddling across the lawns again. But there was concern for these little bundles of feathers. Deep in the university lake lurked a pike and he was seizing these innocent little fluff balls with the ferocity of a shark on the rampage; a vicious swirl of water, a great splash and another baby duck vanished to the wild, plaintive honking of its parents.

The girl students organised petitions to have the carnage stopped and the marauder murdered. That fish cast the only shadow over the summer scene. Students were sunbathing, lying around in scruffy clothes or throwing Frisbees. There were no pretty summer dresses, no Jane Foster-Dunns to sighingly admire flaunting themselves in crisp white linen. It was not the summer scene on campus that I had fondly imagined. Grunge was in and prettiness was out; everyone was still wearing old denims and floppy tee shirts like a uniform.

Where have all the flowers gone?

I sat on the stone steps killing time before the Professor's seminar. All around me students were lying about on the grass. Ants were scurrying from the cracks in the pavement near my feet. I stared at them, wondering which ones were coming and which ones were going. There I was, a giant, looking down on their world. Was someone up there looking down on mine and so on *ad infinitum*?

Now which author would be most likely to develop that train of thought and imagery?

Help, I'm cracking up! This degree course has got me staring at cracks in the pavement!

I went indoors and down the well-grooved corridors and noticed for the first time a series of etchings on the walls. They were of a beautiful woman wearing very little more than a diaphanous veil and a puzzled smile. She was having a curiously interesting time with a swan and the bird was being extremely friendly. Something stirred in the section of my brain marked Classics and I examined the pictures more closely. Of course! It was Leda and that inquisitive swan was Zeus in disguise who was about to have his wicked way with her.

For those with the knowledge these were very naughty pictures indeed. I realised that another academic door had opened up for me: there I was appreciating classical, sophisticated, artistic porn. I paused, looked and guiltily hurried on

The Professor waved us into his lair and did his usual furious domestic circuit, filing papers and slitting open letters, talking all the while. He enthused over Racine's absolutism. What exactly is absolutism?

Before anyone dares to ask he explained rapidly. 'You understand what I say?'

This became his catch phrase. Strangely enough I did. His personality had goaded me into greater concentration and understanding. I invariably sat beside him in the seminar group and he grinned at me sideways, his shock of grey hair and eyebrows making him look like an elderly imp. He was terrifying, but fun as long as you kept your wits about you.

'John! What's this bit mean?'

Oh Lord, it's me again.

'Well . . . '

I waffle for a couple of minutes.

'Ok, but there's more to it than that surely. Jane! What else?'

Jane leaps like a gaffed pike, eyes rolling: 'Perhaps it's about . . . '

'Don't think so,' says the Professor. 'Michael!'

Concentrate! Concentrate! Think! Think!

★ ★ ★

Too much reading! One French play — in French of course, two American books and an essay. Timetable yourself boy!

But the sun shone and the lawns needed cutting. Meriel was kind and understanding, but then a neighbour wandered by and saw me doing 'nothing' with a book in a deck chair while Meriel was nearby on her knees, weeding. 'All right for some,' said the neighbour pointedly.

Don't people realise I am working?

15

A General Election approached, but all the debates and opinion polls bounced off the university's walls as if the outside world did not exist.

Then Stacey was on the phone. As an occasional freelance for ITV, he had been asked to get the results of two of the parliamentary elections in our area. 'How about earning an easy hundred quid for one quick telephone call?' It sounded too good to be true. 'You do one and I'll do the other. We'll be inside for the count and they're putting in special phones.'

That was a blessing for we both remembered the days, long before mobile phones, when we stood outside in the street through the chill hours of the morning, waiting for the results to be announced. Then there was the gallop to the nearest public phone to broadcast the news to the world. This new arrangement sounded much more civilised.

'You're on.'

Despite such a simple sounding operation the pressure slowly grew. Special passes had to be applied for, the counting station at a local school had to be visited to check the layout and arrangements; pages of instructions arrived explaining the exact form in which the result had to be sent.

Watching television it was clear that war had been declared between ITV and BBC, with each claiming that they would provide the fastest results service on the night. On television, I saw that I was to be one of a dedicated nationwide team bringing into every home the fastest election results service ever.

Stacey was on the phone again. 'You'll never guess . . . '

'Tell me.'

'There's a bonus if we get through first with the result. Guess how much?'

'No idea.'

'On top of the hundred, another one hundred and sixty pounds!'

Yorkshire's famous, incredulous response rang out, ''Ow much?'

'You heard.'

I had indeed and I felt the adrenalin building and the tension.

★ ★ ★

'With that sort of money floating around it's going to be cut throat,' I told Meriel. 'Their

144

lads will be on bonuses, too . . . '

It was no longer a lucrative bit of fun. This was getting serious. With the television stations building up the atmosphere on TV, I left home and drove to the polling station, arriving far too early, and parked in the special media car park in the play ground.

I was part of the team! Inside the building one could feel the tension. Rows of tables had unopened ballot boxes piled high, waiting; tellers sat in rows, their fingers itching to be let loose on them; candidates, agents and their helpers, all carrying clipboards, whispered furtively and wandered around checking lists and on the periphery of this edgily moving throng were the media, my rivals. I eyed them and they eyed me. I tested my telephone landline and got a reassuring hum. Please, please stay that way.

The Returning Officer and his helpers finished their counting, checked their lists and the boxes were opened, ballot papers pouring out onto the tables. The count had begun.

From a balcony running around the sports hall I had a perfect view. After a few discreet questions I was able to work out the system and watched the growing piles of votes cast for each candidate.

The hours went by and a deep sense of boredom set in. At one point I found a well-dressed, middle-aged lady standing beside me looking down on the tables.

'Always the worst part,' she said conversationally. 'The waiting . . . '

'Strange job politics,' I said. 'Every five years they have to go through this ritual knowing that tomorrow they could be out of a job.'

'Makes life interesting,' she said in cultured tones.

The conversation meandered pleasantly along over previous election campaigns about which she appeared to know a great deal.

'I'm afraid I don't know your name,' she said eventually.

I introduced myself.

She smiled sweetly, 'I'm the wife of the Conservative candidate.'

'I should have recognised you.' I apologised.

'Not at all. Why should you, I keep a low profile these days. It's been pleasant talking to you. I had better go and circulate among the helpers. Keep up morale.'

'Good luck with the count,' I said as she walked away.

Her response was to gently wave crossed fingers in the air. 'Going all right so far.'

I glanced down at the tables and saw that her ladyship was right. Her husband's pile of votes was enormous compared with those of the other two candidates. At the same time I sensed a stirring among the other reporters. Some were already on their telephones; were they chatting to their wives or to their news desks?

Judging by the piles of votes on the tables the result was a foregone conclusion: the Conservative candidate, who had a safe seat anyway, was already well ahead. Were some of the media, particularly the BBC, going to take a flyer?

I slipped down into the body of the hall and did some quiet checking. All the ballot boxes were in, none had gone missing; this I knew from past experience could cause enormous trouble and delays. And yes, that was the table with all the Conservative votes. I debated with myself: should I, too, be muttering down the telephone? But what if I sent through the result and someone demanded a recount? What if a ballot box had gone missing after all?

I could see the dreadful word 'Correction' flashing up on an imaginary TV screen. But there was a real, large-screen television in the hall for all to see. The premature result would appear on there and any correction. Oh the shame! I could imagine all the young reporters looking round the hall searching for the culprit and all eyes settling on me. Poor old soul, they would say, where on earth did ITV dig him up from? Wherever it was they should have left him buried there.

And then on that same imaginary TV screen I saw £260 signs flashing up and I was assailed with other doubts. Those furtive figures with their phones pressed to their ears decided me: they must be taking a flyer and putting the result through early. What if I were now left so far behind that even my initial payment was put in doubt? I made up my mind and walked to my telephone trying to look indifferent and casual. To the brisk lady at the other end of the line I said, 'Conservatives hold. Votes cast coming in a minute.'

Boats were burned, the Rubicon had been crossed. I could not, at that moment, think of any more literary turning points; they would have to suffice. There was then an agonising wait until the Returning Officer made his announcement and the result was finally confirmed. I made the final phone call and drove home depressed and emotionally exhausted.

★   ★   ★

'We won't get the bonus,' I said to Meriel. 'I'm sure the others sent it through long before I did.'

'Never mind, one hundred pounds is nice.'

'Two hundred and sixty would have been nicer.'

It was not just the money; I felt I had been thrown into the cauldron of my old world and when the chips were down and the pressure was on I had been found wanting. It was a good job I was retired. I was well out of it.

The telephone rang early next morning. 'Hey, hey, hey,' cried Stacey. 'The old guys did it! We beat 'em!'

'Never!'

'You bet your sweet cotton-picking life we did. Cheque for £260 on its way.'

My spirits soared, but then reality crept in. Why was I subjecting myself to all this? For goodness sake, you are retired. Grow up!

★ ★ ★

It was a relief to get back to the Beat generation as part of my American Studies. I vaguely remembered living through this era and as a dyed-in-the-wool traditionalist being totally disparaging about the lot of them; and now they were part of history. In the seminar I asked with pretended naivety, 'Did this Beat scene ever get anywhere?'

I was convinced in my own mind that it had not, but, as I expected, came the usual 'literary reply': it depends what you meant by 'getting anywhere'.

There was a disparaging sniff from Jim, the hippy with the pink Andy Pandy suit, spiky hair and earring; I am sure he identified in spirit with this period of time, but after the sniff came silence.

'Perhaps,' said the lecturer, gently trying to open a discussion, 'Perhaps it is the quest that matters and not the getting anywhere.'

Fiona grinned, 'And the quest can be inside your head!'

Jim decided to contribute, 'And sometimes the journey is stationary, man!'

That stunned the group. Get the grass out everyone and let's fly! Remember to keep an open mind, but what am I doing here?

★   ★   ★

Racine, Molière, and the Beats, weird American poetry, beautiful American poetry ... too much, too much. The end of term came and not before time. I spent the first few weeks of the holiday working on long essays and sorting out books.

'You are supposed to be on holiday!' cried my wife.

'Got to be done, and I'm enjoying it.'

'You don't look as if you're enjoying it.'

'I am, I am.'

'Just take a look at yourself in a mirror. You look ghastly, all washed out. You'll give yourself a heart attack and I'm not picking up that damn degree of yours posthumously. Besides, I don't look good in black.'

Meriel was right yet again. Let's be sensible. I did wonder how the young coped with all this. They were young that was why. And perhaps older students became too obsessed and conscientious.

I put a timetable on the wall with days allocated to different subjects and guiltily marked a few days for 'trips out'.

These involved shopping expeditions into town with Meriel, but my brain was elsewhere. 'I married a zombie,' Meriel concluded, as I confessed that I had completely forgotten where I had parked the car.

Back home Meriel left cups of tea outside the door. I took a few sips and when I picked up the cup again the tea had gone cold. I went out into the garden and walked around, but could not be bothered to sniff the flowers.

Fortunately Meriel had a project, and had become absorbed in The Party: a combination of my birthday and our wedding anniversary celebrations.

On the day, a small marquee with a lot of attitude appeared on the lawn and some fifty people arrived. It was a great party: noisy, jolly and crowded. I ran through the same conversation with several people, always trying to be self-denigrating about being at university.

The loudest laughs came from a circle of women around John Jackson a fellow journalist, middle-aged, mischief-eyed, bald as a balloon, yet the women were around him like flies after strawberry jam. He grinned at me as I went by on my rounds. His wife, a handsome, vivacious woman was engrossed with the East African reminiscences of my Samaritan friend Harry. And there was Meriel's cousin, just turned forty and dying of cancer and he knew it. Why? Why? There's that age-old question again. Is the only answer really a hippopotamus?

Cousin Ian who made a speech at our wedding forty years ago made one now and so did I. The words had been going round in my head for days, but they did not come out in the right order; they never do, but nobody seemed to mind. The party went happily on.

Time passed and people went home in the small hours; there was a silence and a sudden emptiness as if it had never been. I was beginning to notice this more and more. Everything was happening faster and faster and everything that was happening stayed for a shorter and shorter period of time before it disappeared into a longer and longer past. I wished I could grab hold of some of those moments and make them stay a little longer, to be savoured.

Meriel cut into the mournful reverie. 'Do you know what people were saying about you?'

'I don't know how he does it?' I suggested hopefully.

'Don't kid yourself. No they didn't. They all said how drawn and tired you looked. This blasted degree is making you ill!'

16

On holiday in France in our farmhouse *gîte* I read Molière and Racine every night. I thought I was becoming schizophrenic. Every time I thought of something in English I tried, and usually failed, to translate it into French. I was obsessed with the fear that I was going to fail this French paper disastrously and make a fool of myself. My brain was beginning to squeak.

We drove through an old French village with a castle-like chateau perched on a crag. In the square was a statue of a happy lady wielding a quill pen. It was Madame de Sevigne! I had been reading about her, she was one of, if not *the* finest letter-writer in history. And there she was penning a letter to her daughter in Provence and recounting all the gossip from the Sun King's court at Versailles. She had lived here; she was a real person not just a name in a book. I wondered what she would have thought if she had known her chatty letters were still being read four hundred years later? Aristocratically appalled at the intrusion into her private world no doubt.

At Aix, I saw an old bookshop in one of the town's narrow back streets. It looked scruffy, dirty and undiscovered. The volumes started in piles on the floor, climbed up rickety shelves and, I swear, seemed to be leaning out at the top as if trying to colonise the ceiling. An old man sat in the middle of this chaos in a battered, moth-eaten armchair.

This was wonderful. Here I would buy a venerable French tome from a venerable French bookseller; something that I would treasure for the rest of my life. 'Have you?' I asked slowly in my careful French. 'Have you *The Letters of Madame de Sevigne?*'

He slowly came to life. Awareness quickened in his face. I detected something akin to pleasure, even joy, flickering in his eyes. I facetiously wondered if he had known the old girl personally.

'Madame de Sevigne!' he cried.

'*Oui.*'

'Madame de Sevigne!'

'*Oui, oui,*' I said excitedly.

'*Non, non,*' he said sadly and collapsed back into his arm chair.

How one's dreams are shattered.

I had to wait for a scout jumble sale in the village hall before I met Madame de Sevigne again. There she was, in English and in a scruffy, well thumbed paperback. Where were the joy and the nostalgia to be had in that?

★ ★ ★

Back at 'school' there was a new mood among our year. I sensed that after casually attending lectures and even more casually putting in essays too late or not at all, the approaching exams had become a dark cloud on the horizon that could no longer be ignored. University life was becoming serious.

After swotting through four plays by Molière and four by Racine the Professor let it be known that the exam questions and translations would cover all of them; in other words we could concentrate on just one play from each playwright. Only at the end of course did he tell us this, so I devised a cunning plan! I wrote two all purpose essays covering my chosen plays. They brought in every possible theme, mood, historical reference, and language analysis that I could squeeze out of my notes and memory. I sat at home, stop-watch ticking, and practised writing out each essay in long-hand.

I woke up in the middle of the night with the essays going round and round in my head like a bad dream. I had never worked so hard or been so worried about the approach of any of the other exams.

Why? I concluded that I felt vulnerable in another language, but above all I wanted to do well for this shock-haired professor with the quicksilver brain; I wanted to impress him. What a childish naïve thought!

★ ★ ★

Then fortunately for my sanity the family arrived. There was a week of glorious chasing about and all thoughts of university were pushed to one side. The early mornings started with the thump, thump of nappyclad legs running along the landing.

'Morning time, g'an'dad! I jump on you!' said James, and he did.

I chased around the garden with him, but retreated into the study with Monsieur Molière while James was force fed 'dunky egg' in the kitchen.

'G'an'dad! G'an'dad! Where's G'an'dad?'

I could hear the cry.

'Granddad is busy.'

'I want g'an'dad!'

Granddad obeys.

For goodness sake! I have only one grandson and he is growing up fast. Monsieur Molière can wait. Strange how often bits of life recall and reawaken bits of poetry. I remembered a poem called *The Gardener* by R L Stevenson. In it the children cannot understand why the gardener wastes his time sweeping up leaves when he could be doing something much more important, like playing games with them.

Well now and while the summer stays
To profit by these garden days,
O how much wiser you would be
To play at Indian wars with me!

My sentiments entirely, Robert Louis! Right on, boy! One of Penny's friends, now grown up, once told me, 'When we were kids we never thought of you as an adult; you were always one of us.'

It brought a lump to my throat whenever I remembered it and I took it as a huge compliment.

But Meriel was not so sure. 'Oh come on, Peter Pan. Grow up!'

★　★　★

It was my monthly check-up at the doctors and I was on edge. Surely my blood pressure would be sky high. But no, it was normal. When I expressed surprise the

158

doctor laughed and said that my feeling on edge was just student nerves. Perhaps he was right.

I lay in bed, with Meriel gently snoring, while I gazed at the ceiling with those two French essays still going round and round in my head like ferrets in a hen run. Student nerves at my age!

The day of the dreaded French exam came and I went off to 'school' clutching my pens and ruler and a packet of mints.

'Good luck, Dad,' said my daughter, trying and failing to suppress a grin. This was role reversal indeed.

'You will be all right,' said my wife briskly. 'Just don't drink too much tea before hand.'

Ever practical Meriel. Oh the shame of having to be escorted to the loo in the middle of a closed exam! The looks, the whispers. 'There he goes, poor old thing. He's probably incontinent!'

★　★　★

A nervous crowd is gathered on the steps leading down to the lecture room. In we go, bags, holdalls and coats dumped in an Oxfam heap at the back. The invigilators are an unsmiling group of lecturers we have not seen before; obviously no risk of favouritism here.

'You may turn over your question paper, now!'

Yippee! I know the Racine selection backwards.

Oh help! The Molière piece is a bitch!

Three hours later I pin all the papers into the folder provided. All those weeks of work and study have come down to eight pages.

For the first time I read the instructions on the front of the exam paper. I never was one for reading instructions; I regarded that as cheating. It was more fun to find out what to do for oneself; treat life as a challenge and a puzzle without taking clues from a crib sheet. But there it was in capital letters: 'Write on both sides of the paper.' I had, in true journalistic fashion, used only one side of the paper.

So just this once who cared about the rain forests! It was over! I was finished with French authors! I could read books in English again. I could burn my French dictionary. Well, perhaps that was going too far.

* * *

'You look ghastly,' said Meriel.

'Thank you.'

'All piggy eyed.'

160

'And I think you look lovely, too.'
'How long is this going on for?'
'The next lot should be easier.'
She sniffed. Meriel had a very expressive sniff.

17

Julien approached at speed; we had not seen much of each other lately as we were on different courses. 'Have you heard? Richard and Anna have split up.'

We retired to his room to discuss the news and he dispensed tea. The mugs were just as grimy and the pile of vegetables under the sink seemed to have grown larger; some I believed had taken root and others were definitely sprouting.

'I gather he dumped her, but she's not talking to me for some reason.'

'Ah well,' I said, not knowing what to say.

'I don't know why she's miffed with me.'

'Probably thinks you would be on Richard's side.'

'I'm not on anyone's side! How can I be? I don't know what's happened.'

We both shook our heads and concluded that we needed to know more, before we passed judgement. Perhaps Richard would be more forthcoming, but without any more first hand information the topic faltered.

After a contemplative silence, the conversation switched to the forthcoming exams.

Julien had decided that he was not going to get a First. No one had told him so, but he knew. And I knew that I was not going to get one either. We had both made our own assessments, measuring ourselves instinctively against the high flyers; no one had been indelicate enough to tell us what we all might achieve, and that I thought was quite clever. We were never set one against the other: the commendable objective appeared to be to make everyone reach their own potential without envying or fearing anyone else's progress. Julien and I both felt content with our self-assessment. Let's hope we were not deluding ourselves. Replete with tea, I wandered back through the college and walked straight into Anna.

'John, have you heard?' she cried. 'How do I look? Do I look awful?'

Considering the situation I thought the question a little odd. 'You look fine.'

'I'm not going to give him the satisfaction of seeing that I'm bothered,' she said defiantly.

But there were tears in her eyes and the alarm bells in my head started ringing in triple majors. Incredulously, I heard myself suggesting a cup of tea and a chat. We sat in one of the snack bars, one nervous elderly gentleman and this beautiful Italian girl with darkly flowing hair and eyes now flowing with tears. I could see heads turning.

This is what my daughter and my wife said I should not be doing.

'Why has he done it? He finished with me! He said it wouldn't work.'

I was puzzled, too. It was girls like Anna who usually did the dumping and it must have come as a formidable shock for her self-esteem to have the tables reversed.

'Would it have worked out?' I said warily.

'It was the social thing,' she murmured. 'I'm sure that was it.'

She was probably right. Richard, I knew, had spent part of the summer in Italy with Anna's family who, I suspected, enjoyed a very high lifestyle. Clever though he was, perhaps Richard had been overawed. Anna's assessment appeared sensible enough to me, but I said nothing.

'We could have worked it out. We got on so well.' Her forefinger, like a demented woodpecker, was battering the ash off a cigarette.

It was then that I had disturbing images of drug overdoses, bodies floating in the lake and sharp questions from the coroner: 'Knowing the young lady's state of mind, did you not think you should have . . . '

'Look,' I said firmly, trying not to sound

too father-like, 'You'll be fine. These things happen . . . Now you're not going to do anything silly are you?'

I cursed myself as soon as the words escaped my lips. I should not have said that! It was all from listening to Harry talking about the Samaritans.

'I feel so lonely,' cried Anna and the tears fell faster.

'Friends are the answer. Go out with your girl-friends. Talk it all over with them. They'll put it in perspective for you. Then you'll feel better.'

Anna sniffed defiantly, 'I'm not giving up male company just because of him.'

I smiled to myself. Wrong again: this was no candidate for a suicide's grave.

'All right then. Pick the next eligible young man in the queue. That'll show Richard! But don't do anything stupid there either.'

Whoops! I should not have said that either! That was another foot firmly in the bog. Now I really was sounding like a worried father.

'I tell you what,' I said, pressing on hurriedly, 'there's a great way you can get your own back on Richard. He thinks he's so clever. Why don't you get yourself a First, that'll show him!'

I was subjected to the full luminosity of those lovely, dark eyes and I could see that the thought of social and academic revenge had fallen on very fertile ground indeed.

'Thank you so much for listening. It's so awful. I can't go home and talk to my parents and it's not the same over the phone.'

How right she was. I remembered the tearful phone calls from my own daughter when she was first at university and that memory helped me launch another more substantial lifeboat into this emotional storm.

'You must get yourself sorted out for your parents' sake. They will be worried sick about you if you start talking to them on the phone in this state.'

Anna was now far, far way.

'Poor Daddy.'

The word 'Daddy' coming from this sophisticated young woman pulled me up short.

★ ★ ★

'Well you have done it now,' said Meriel. 'What are people going to think, you talking to a weeping girl, and in public! Honestly! Have you no common sense at all? Let her sort out her own affairs. It's none of your business.'

'I'm not involved.'

'Of course you are involved.'

'Well so what if I am?' I said angrily. 'What should I have said to her? 'Hard luck, darling, pull yourself together?' Very sympathetic and helpful that would be. Remember that university girl down south who was in the papers? She hanged herself over some boyfriend, do you remember that? 'No one to talk to,' she said in her suicide note.'

'Don't be so dramatic. Anna's not going to commit suicide. She's far too sensible. You just like getting involved, don't you? Makes you feel important.'

And after that tirade I started sheepishly to examine my motives. Might my dear wife be right?

★　★　★

And then the next day there was Richard. 'What did she say to you?'

Clearly someone had seen the tearful tea party and told him. I wondered uneasily how far that report had spread.

'She was very upset,' I said vaguely.

'She thinks it's the class thing. But it isn't.'

'Indeed.'

'She was always pushing me to do this and that; planning my whole life for me, she was . . . Organising everything . . . Telling me I should be more authoritative. But that's just not me. I couldn't put up with it any longer.'

'Probably all for the best then?'

'Probably.'

But he still looked miserable.

And then with all the slick timing of a French farce, as soon as Richard disappeared there was Anna.

'What did he say? What did he say?'

Meriel was right, I was involved, but now I was determined to extricate myself. I was not going to be pushed into the role of a go-between, someone who would inevitably be shot at and despised by both sides.

'He is upset,' I said guardedly.

'Upset! Why is he upset! He finished with me!'

I gestured helplessly feeling trapped between them.

'I went to see him, you know,' said Anna. 'Tried to sort it out. We ended up having another terrible row. He said I was too bossy . . . Always trying to organise him. Couldn't he see I was only trying to help! I want him to get a life.'

I noticed a smartly dressed young man watching us.

'I think someone wants to talk to you,' I said, hoping to break off the discussion, but with barely a glance in his direction Anna dismissed the young man's presence with an impatient flick of the head.

'Ignore him! Why is Richard upset? It doesn't make sense.'

'I'm sure he was very fond of you,' I suggested.

'Then why did he do this!'

Richard had honestly given Anna his answer to that one, but it was not for me to underline it, nor thankfully was it necessary. Anna talked and talked and I listened and tried to be sympathetic, which I genuinely was. My final contribution was to murmur, 'I'm sure things will work themselves out.'

★ ★ ★

'That's it!' I firmly told Meriel. 'I am not involved,'

'Hah!'

169

18

Everyone crowded into another lecture by Dr P. His fame had spread among us, but for me there was an added incentive. We were studying the literature surrounding the English Civil War, a gory time full of raging political and religious conflicts and above all battles; and it was in these that I had always taken a perhaps unhealthy interest. I was not alone. In my working days, I had got to know Peter, a historian and lecturer at the local teacher training college. He was a historic battle enthusiast and had founded a re-enactment group. When it came to retelling old battles the man was a joy for someone like me; standing in the calm tranquillity of Marston Moor among the grazing sheep he would, with sweeping arms and rolling phrases, paint word-pictures so vivid that you could almost see Cromwell's Roundheads sweeping down the hill, hear the crackle of musket-fire and see the steady, terrifying advance of the pikemen, like a deadly steel tipped hedge on the move.

Peter's Civil War re-enactments were famous and always included a little cameo

involving himself. Flourishing his extrava-
gantly feathered hat in one hand and his
sword in the other, he would lead the charge
only to be wounded in the first exchange of
fire. Staggering gallantly on before collapsing,
he would lift himself up on one elbow and
wave his troops forwards before collapsing
again. His personal guard, all strapping,
costume-clad girl students from the college,
would then carry him from the field on a
stretcher to appreciative cheers from the
audience. Peter always survived to fight
another day.

So thanks to him I knew all about the
battles and thanks to Dr P I learned
something of the wonderful words that went
with them. But first, Dr P, in his inimitable
way, filled in some history about Charles II, a
man, he said, with a reputation for bravery.

'However, his only achievement on that
score was to climb and hide in a tree, the
Royal Oak, to the everlasting satisfaction of
the English Hoteliers Association.'

And as an aside we were told that the king
had fourteen children, not one of them
legitimate, and their mothers had all been
made duchesses.

'Most of the English aristocracy,' Dr P said
to our denigrating delight, 'is descended from
the great bastardy of Charles II.'

And having got our rapt attention we were painlessly led into the literature of the period, the poetry, the letters, the propaganda leaflets and the parliamentary speeches. Cromwell, as well as being a ruthless soldier, had a wicked way with words; what a journalist he would have made. His battle descriptions were vividly vicious: 'God made them as stubble to our swords,' he wrote.

And then there was the brusque, heart-stopping letter to the father of one of his officers killed at Marston Moor: 'Sir, God hath taken away your eldest son by a cannon-shot. It broke his leg. We were necessitated to have it cut off, whereof he died ... the Lord took him into the happiness we all pant after and live for. There is your precious child full of glory, to know sin nor sorrow any more. He was a gallant young man, exceeding gracious. God give you His comfort.'

That part of the letter leapt off the paper and disturbed me. I fell to wondering how many thousands of such letters had been written by officers to grieving parents down the centuries. All of them must have conveyed the same devastating news, perhaps in gentler tones, but surely there was never another letter written with such emotional power.

And then I remembered my supervisor's

advice to read the text again and I got another shock; that powerful piece of prose came in the middle of Cromwell's letter. At its start Cromwell detailed the course of the battle and the gallant part he, himself, had played in the victory; only then did he get round to telling the recipient that his son was dead. So apart from being a powerful piece of writing the letter opened a revealing window into the complex personality of a man whom even his enemies called 'a brave bad man'.

★ ★ ★

I kept my distance from Anna, but even from afar a change in her behaviour and attitude was obvious. She was even more glamorously groomed and had gathered about her a small 'court' of girls among whom stood out the well dressed young man, accepted it seemed as an occasional courtier. Richard appeared preoccupied and lost in his own world of books.

I was more than happy to leave it that way, but then I met Anna striding across the campus. We came face to face and I could not ignore her. 'Hi,' I said cheerfully.

'I've taken your advice. David is taking me out.'

My advice? I quailed at the thought. Yes I

suppose I had stupidly given some advice, but I was startled to hear that it had been acted upon. David, I assumed, was the well-dressed young man.

'Good.'

Anna looked at me archly.

'And he is being a perfect gentleman.'

That look told me very clearly indeed that I had gone too far with my fatherly advice.

'But,' she said, and there was an arch look on her face, 'I get the feeling that he would like the relationship to progress.'

I was being gently teased.

'Glad everything is sorted,' I said and went on my way. I had become involved and it really had been none of my business. I reflected on the emotional life of students: one moment they behaved like young, vulnerable children and the next they were all cool and terrifyingly grownup. What was an old man in their midst to make of them? Keep your distance perhaps. Meriel had been right: they could and would sort out their own affairs. But had I helped just by listening? Perhaps, perhaps not, who knows? I comforted myself by thinking that no one I knew would be found floating Ophelia-like in the lake.

★ ★ ★

There was tension in the air at home. It had started with my 'involvement' with Anna, but the irritation grew. I kept forgetting things, like picking up a pound of tomatoes on the way home or putting petrol in the car.

'If it's anything to do with me or the house you just don't want to know, do you?' said Meriel, when I again forgot to pick up something vital to the household management.

'You're not on this planet half the time. Do you ever see the jobs that have to be done round here? No you don't, because I do them all. I'm just running a bed and breakfast establishment here for your own personal convenience. You do absolutely nothing, you just eat, sleep and vanish!'

'We'll go out for a meal,' I said humbly.

'Are you sure you can spare the time?'

We did eat out and happily the mood changed for the best until . . . Meriel had been reading cruise brochures and I kept finding them lying around the house with trips circled in pencil.

'Monarch of the Seas,' said Meriel one night. 'Have we been on that boat?'

'We have not been on that *boat*,' I said, heavily emphasising the last word.

'I'm sure we have.'

'We have not been on that *boat*, but we

have been on that *ship*.'

'What!'

'Ships carry boats. The captain would be most upset if you called his ship a boat.'

There was an explosion.

'Ship! Boat! What the Hell's the difference! You know exactly what I'm talking about. I'm sick to death of your pedantic nitpicking. I wonder I have any confidence left the way you go on. You're not the man I married, and I'll tell you something else, if you had gone on like this when I first met you I never would have married you.'

That outburst came as a shock. I honestly did not realise that I was doing it, but it was true, I was always questioning the use of words and phrases. Such hypercriticism was all right in the seminar room, but not in domestic life.

This, coming on top of everything else, would have to stop. I was going to have to watch my tongue very carefully and do more at home. I had to get at least one foot back on planet earth, preferably two, so I could push the lawnmower.

And just at that moment Stacey telephoned and suggested a coffee *rendez-vous*. I immediately felt guilty; here I was again disappearing and this time not for 'work' but just to enjoy myself.

'Go!' said Meriel. 'Talk to some real people for a change. Get yourself off Cloud Nine or wherever it is you're floating around on at the moment.'

And that made for a rather subdued journey to our usual coffee haunt.

★ ★ ★

'Heard any good ones lately?' was Stacey's greeting. In our glory days, when every organisation in our town held annual dinners and dances, the pair of us were *the* young men about town attending all the social functions. The Lord Mayor slipped us copies of his speeches and the Lord Mayor's butler ensured that our wine glasses were topped up no matter how far down the festive board we were sitting. The butler, a grand red-coated figure, would drift by, expertly filling our glasses while murmuring for all to hear, 'With the compliments of the Lord Mayor.' Our neighbouring guests were very impressed. Apart from recording the speeches of community leaders on the controversies of the day, Stacey and I collected the after-dinner jokes. We had a fund of them and Stacey's query was an echo of those happy days.

I shook my head sadly. 'Nothing.'

'Me neither.'

'Not been anywhere to hear any.'

'Me neither.'

And that was it. We both felt like yesterday's men: no deadlines, no important events to dash to, and no new jokes to pass on.

'Getting the holiday organised,' said Stacey. 'Looking forward to it — a trip through the Rockies. Three weeks . . . '

Was that what our conversation had dwindled down to? We who were once the fount of knowledge on all local topics were reduced to discussing the organisation of our holidays.

I had never given holidays much thought since our visit to France, which had been a thinly disguised attempt to brush up my French before the exams. Stacey was full of the detailed arrangements for his holiday and that stirred still further my fermenting feelings of guilt. I should at least have shown a glimmer of interest in all those cruises carefully ringed in the brochures.

19

Suddenly I felt lonely at university. It was the dissertation term, which did not require seminars, tutorial groups or even any lectures to break the silence. And the subject matter of my dissertation did nothing to lighten the spirits. I had always been morbidly fascinated by the First World War and my research plunged me into abyss-depths of gloom and despair.

'I don't want to hear any more thank you,' said Meriel crisply, as I tried to share another piece of horror from Robert Graves.

'Why did the Second World War not produce the high literature of the First?' was my theme. Ye gods! If writers could not produce literature out of all that innocent loyalty and decency flowing into a pit of senseless carnage, then all those poets and writers should have been shot: come to think of it many of them were, but not for lack of literary inspiration.

I struggled on with forays to the library for more books, and there were nods from familiar faces buried in their own dissertation work. Everyone was isolated, locked into his or her own little world. This, said the university syllabus, was an opportunity for deep, sustained individual research, but I began to doubt if 'deep, sustained individual research' was my style of garret. I preferred the chat and social exchanges of seminars and tutorials. Strange how my early university years were already developing a rosy glow of nostalgia and I had not yet left the place.

At last, a social link with a human being. I saw my dissertation tutor for a midterm check on progress. He lived in a distant part of the campus, so I had to tramp down new corridors, past new posters and into an alien atmosphere. I had been winkled out of my own cosy corner, with its familiar friendly faces and I felt uneasy. My dissertation tutor was pleasant enough, large and untidy. He reminded me of a sub-editor on one of my early newspapers who kept his red setter dog under the sub editors' table. 'It's a big subject you've chosen. I would concentrate on one or two books.'

'Which ones?' Stupid man! Do you really expect to get an answer to that sort of question?

'That's your choice,' was the obvious answer. 'Which ones had you in mind?'

I mentioned two or three.

'No one would quarrel with those.'

That, I thought, was a nod of approval.

'And from the Second World War?'

I mentioned some authors and he pursed his lips.

'You seem to be on the right lines. I'm sure it will be an excellent dissertation. I look forward to reading it.'

You and me both, sunshine, I said to myself.

I walked back along the unfamiliar corridors and across the bridge over the lake to my own part of 'town'.

★ ★ ★

In the snack bar, Julien came rushing across. He was in a state of shock. 'Have you heard about Richard?'

Richard? What had happened to him? More to the point, was I in any way responsible?

'What's he done?' I demanded, dreading to hear the answer. I had never anticipated any dramatic emotional reaction from sensible Richard.

'He's got married!'

That, too, I did not expect. Surely there had not been a passionate reconciliation with Anna culminating in a rush to the Registry Office. I could not believe it and I was right. Richard had married someone else, a shy, sweet little blonde girl whom he had met at the beginning of the term.

'I gather his parents are furious,' said Julien.

I was not surprised

'What does Anna say?'

'I don't know what Anna says and I'm certainly not going to ask.'

We both fell silent. I was glad that, after all, it was dissertation term. What would have happened if all those involved in this romantic little soap opera had to meet and work together in seminars and tutorial groups? At least everyone could come to terms with the new situation in relative isolation.

★   ★   ★

Anna vanished from sight, but I met Richard and his wife and offered my congratulations. She was charming, not as shy as she had first appeared, though Richard stood beside her with a protective arm around her shoulder. I asked how the exams were going and got the usual self-deprecating reply. I thought they made a more compatible couple than Richard and Anna, but who was I to judge? The deed was done.

The mood among 'our' students was

changing. I overheard conversations in the coffee bars comparing rejection letters and non-replies. After nearly three years of relatively carefree days, life was becoming serious for them all over again. Julien had decided he wanted to be a barrister and was sounding out the London law schools. He was excited and not without reason, a whole new world was opening out for him; life's great adventure was beginning. I had a shameful twinge of envy. No great life adventure was waiting for me.

★ ★ ★

During this term of 'sustained individual research' I found time to devote some critical thought to the university's examination system. As a very mature student, I was full of admiration. I would have folded my tent and departed long ago if all the nodules had been closed exams — those horrible, sweat inducing, three hour long memory tests. There had been some of those and there were some yet to come, crammed into the last few weeks, but most of the subjects had been examined as we went along and in a variety of ways. Often the work was done by course essays or long essays, many with six months to prepare and write. No one could claim that they had not had time or opportunity to display fully their learning or lack of it.

I submitted my dissertation: 10,000 words neatly typed and in a plastic file. At least the presentation looked impressive. But all my old fears surfaced as I handed it in. Should I have made it boring just to prove my seriousness? Or made it more obscure to suggest a mind full of deep, dark complexities too profound for mere words to capture? Should I have indulged in more problematisation of every idea?

And yet some of the best lecturers had made things appear brilliantly simple, but they were brilliant people to start with. Come on, forget it! It's over, finished with. Move on.

A burden the weight of a mountain fell away.

★ ★ ★

Easter holidays and then the last term of my university life began. Those final, dreaded, closed written exams were approaching. I read until my eyes came out on stalks and Meriel became even more worried. She went quiet, apart from asking repeatedly when it would all end. I was sure she had visions of a sudden heart attack dramatically ending it all.

Back on the campus the atmosphere had

changed totally; we stood in anxious groups around notice boards to gather exam dates. They were well spaced out, thank heavens, so again I prepared wall charts and time tables. I selected lecture notes, chose my best essays and put them into revision files. I practised writing answers on general topics, but there was no all-purpose essay that could possibly cover Shakespeare and his contemporaries.

'The questions will be on literary themes,' said the rubric. Was this helpful? I read madly on themes: love, jealousy, kingship — gathering in a sheaf of ready quotations.

The exams came and the exams went; days of pen-clutching tension and self-questioning. Why was I putting myself through this at my age?

Did the university know how to cope with a heart attack in the middle of a closed exam?

For me the normal, outside world ceased to exist; my every thought, waking and sleeping, was churning around the next piece of revision until, at last, there was only one big exam left.

All our year was taking this one. I headed for the Central Hall, seeing the trickle of fellow students moving across the lawns, along the walkways and over the bridge. Always looking for an apt simile, I thought they were ant-like, but then I changed my mind; no, not ant-like, we lacked the ants' urgency and sense of purpose. Shakespeare, as usual, had got it spot on: 'snail-like, unwillingly to school.' That fitted us perfectly.

My poor brain should not have been taxing itself with such trivia; it was already so overloaded with quotations that it was in danger of exploding.

The floor area of the vast Central Hall was filled with desks and the stage was filled with lecturers. The sheer scale of this examination setup was terrifying. Faces smiled nervously in greeting. Julien looked very hangdog and twitchy. We all picked up our desk numbers and filed into place, like dumb sheep sorted for shearing.

The clock ticked. I put a row of unwrapped mints on my desk and wondered if it were good for my heart to be thumping like this at my age?

I breathed slowly and deeply. Why was I here? What if my mind went blank? What if I could not remember a thing?

'You may now look at your papers.'

Oh no! There were no questions at all, just a series of passages from books and plays . . . 'Expand on the themes hidden in these passages.'

How could three hours go so quickly? I finished and checked through my writing.

It was awful! Was that all I could find to say about the most glorious and exciting period of English literature? I was deflated, depressed and downright annoyed with myself. I could have done better, much better. I offered up silent thanks that all the exams had not been like this.

The bell tolled and there was a rumble of shuffling feet; aching shoulder muscles were stretched and a collective sigh was released. Julien was looking sick. 'I have never written so much unmitigated rubbish in my life,' he whispered.

'Me, too.'

The depression slowly lifted as students poured out into the sunshine and onto the lawns by the lake. It was not possible to be depressed for long when the sun was shining on green grass and those ridiculous ducks were waddling and a'quacking.

All right it had been terrible, but that was the last one! The very last one! It was over! We all had that bewildered, dazed look of freshly released prisoners blinking in the sunlight.

The highfliers exchanged quick grins and thumbs-up signs, 'Not too bad,' they said confidently. 'Told you there would be a question on masques.'

Smug devils, I hated them. No I did not. I

really did not. Well done and good luck to them!

Sarah flicked back her long hair and the gesture no longer looked gauche and nervous, but rather fetching. She had got a job teaching English in Japan.

Released from the tension of the exam room they all seemed to have changed, becoming relaxed and more self-confident.

The jungle telegraph sent a message through the chattering groups hanging about aimlessly outside the Central Hall and there was a surge towards the village pub. I joined them; after all, it was for the last time.

The place was packed, but sitting around the beer-slopped tables no one quite knew what to say. They were all still sober and I guessed that as the day wore on the gatherings would become much noisier affairs. But at that moment there was just a stunned awareness that it was over. Those long, lazy university days that would fill the rest of their lives with nostalgic memories had gone; they had slipped away like the last grains of sand from the hourglass.

I looked at them all around the table and at the relief and eagerness on all their faces. A brave new world was out there waiting for them to explore.

* ★ *

I drove home in a daze. No more seminars, no more tutorials, no more wrestling with essays. The mountain that had stood in my path had been scaled and I stood on its summit and looked out, but at what? What was out there waiting for me? Anything? Anything at all?

It was like leaving work and retiring all over again.

Meriel sensed the mood and had eminently practical solutions as usual. 'If you've nothing to do, the hall has to be decorated. I haven't mentioned it before, but you will have to sort out that damp patch first.'

'Damp patch'? What damp patch?

I had been dallying with Shakespeare, my head full of the religious upheavals of the 17th century, the poetry of Wyatt and the soaring cadenzas of Milton. What was all this about a damp patch?

'And if you want a job outside, that front hedge is a disgrace.'

What front hedge? We've got a front hedge?

I sat in the spare bedroom and looked at the files adorning the shelves. Good Grief! Did I really start to learn Anglo-Saxon? That seemed years ago. And Chaucer — that vast thick book where my thumb was permanently stuck in the glossary at the back; and then there were those American poets and those Greek plays.

I started putting copies of essays into neat heaps, and the copies of the long essays into still more files. A little voice kept saying, 'Why?' But I could not abandon all that work to the dustbin — not yet.

Meriel saw me buried in papers, 'Where are you putting those?'

'Not sure yet.'

'Do you really need them?'

'I might.'

'What for?'

'I don't know.'

'I'll get you a box and you can put them up in the attic. If you really have to keep them.'

Up in the attic? Up amongst the old toys, the unwanted bits of carpet and my collection of old tennis rackets that might be valuable some day? Was all that work to be despatched to the attic so soon? But what was I keeping it for?

I looked at the heap of essays. If laid end to end, how far would they stretch? Who cares?

I went downstairs and stared at the damp patch in the hall. Had my world really narrowed down to this?

20

I was invited to the graduates' drinks party given by the English Department as a farewell to its students. I dreamed of entering a mellow, learned Oxbridge ambience and had visions of a candlelit evening in the old Elizabethan hall, which was the only venerable part of the new university. I was sadly disappointed. We met in daylight in one of the shabby seminar rooms; there were no candles and panelled walls, just a few crates of wine and glasses piled on a table in the corner. It was difficult to summon up much nostalgia for the end of our university days.

Defiantly, I wore what I considered normal attire for the event, a tie and jacket, and for once I did not care how conspicuous I looked. A few of the academic staff had been rounded up to socialise, but the atmosphere was subdued; for them it was probably an end of the year ritual that had become a chore. A photographer arrived and took a group photograph; another collection of faces to be stuck on a wall somewhere, carefully dated and eventually forgotten. Wine glasses were drained and the party broke up. Duty done, thank you and goodbye, next intake please.

★   ★   ★

At home, I found some university books that I had forgotten to return so I took them back to the library and had a farewell chat with the nice ladies behind the counter.

'Will you miss us?' said one of them.

'I'm missing you already,' I said and they laughed.

'You could stop on and do a Master of Arts,' said another of them. 'Lots of the older students do that.'

A higher degree! I did not even know yet if I had got a lower one. But the grandiose idea of becoming a Master of Arts had already flickered across my mind. I could have been very tempted to delve into the propaganda leaflet battle that had raged during the English Civil War. Goebbels, the Nazi propaganda minister in World War Two could have learned a thing or two from those Roundheads and Cavaliers; when they put quill to paper and cranked up the printing press, their battle-reporting skills were worthy of deeper study. Yes, I could happily wallow in that world for another year.

But then I told myself firmly to stop

daydreaming. Had I forgotten so quickly? I had only just been released from the rack. Did I seriously want to climb back onto it again? And what about Meriel having someone in her house who was always plugged into another world? Could I seriously put her through all that again? No, enough was enough for everyone's sanity.

I made my farewells to the library staff and stood on the library steps looking down on the campus buildings stretching down the hill and I wondered where to go. There was no need for me to go anywhere, but as I was there I wandered over to the English Department. The notice board was full of information about careers and working holidays.

The Professor came crashing out of his office reading a sheaf of papers; he looked up, waved cheerily and dashed off down the corridor. He was lost in another world in which I was no longer even a name on a piece of paper. I drank a lonely cup of tea in the snack bar. All 'my year' had gone home long ago.

Get yourself home, too, you silly old fool.

Something else in my life had come and gone and here I was trying to hang onto it.

Let it go, it was over, finished with, already just a memory.

★ ★ ★

'How do you think you've done?'

The question came at me repeatedly, but with slightly more serious interest from my teacher friends who, I suspected, thought I would have perished by the wayside long ago. 'Going to dazzle us all with a First?' said Marion yet again.

'No chance at all. You can tell the Firsts and I am not of their number.'

★ ★ ★

The weeks dragged by.

I felt in limbo, unable to settle to anything. Eventually we were told when the results would be posted on the notice boards. The day before Julien rang. He and his friends would be milling around the office as soon as the doors opened. Did I want him to let me know my results? No thank you. I would take my shocks at first hand and in my own good time.

That morning I cut the lawns and half-heartedly weeded the flower beds, conscious that Meriel was watching and saying nothing.

Over a more or less silent lunch she suddenly said, 'So when are you going, then?'

'Soon.'

★ ★ ★

I drove slowly to the university. What if it was a Third? I could imagine the eager requests for information from friends and then the enforced, 'Oh well done! That's still a degree isn't it?'

I distracted myself by picturing a scene of Greek tragedy around the department notice board: young maidens wailing and rending their garments; youths leaping into the stairwell or falling on their biros. But it was all very calm; the early morning causalities had been carted away.

I edged through the small crowd to view the neatly-typed lists. There were only a few Firsts and the first one was Anna. I could not believe it. She whom the lecturers hated; she who could not express herself in English; she against whom the whole world conspired had got a First?

Richard had got one, too, which was expected, and several others who had shone like beacons among our dim rays. But Anna!

Momentarily I had a shaming feeling of resentment. Come on, granddad was this just because she was a girl? A woman had done better than you? Come on! Good luck to her, but really, Anna of all people!

I continued down the list into the Two

195

One's and there I was. I had got a Two One.

I took a deep, deep breath. I had got a Two One. I was now BA (Hons) Eng. Lit.

I looked for Julien's name and there he was: another Two One. I felt almost as delighted for him as I did for myself; he needed the qualification and I did not.

I checked further, noting names from our seminar groups. They all seemed to have come through.

★ ★ ★

'I got a Two One,' I told Meriel on the phone. 'Well done!'

But as usual she sensed something.

'You're not disappointed with that surely?'

'Anna got a First,' and as soon as I said it I felt like a little boy pouting, because someone had got a bigger lollypop.

'Good for her,' said Meriel briskly. 'And well done, you. Get yourself home and we'll start ringing round. Penny will be thrilled.'

★ ★ ★

The local paper wanted to take a picture of me in cap and gown.

'How about cap and gown with young grandson?' I said to the News Editor.

'Great!' he said down the telephone and he sounded genuinely enthusiastic.

I remembered that I was good at sounding enthusiastic on telephones. Penny used to listen to me in full flow and shake her head. 'Old velvet-tonsils is at it again,' she would say.

★　★　★

The euphoria and the smug feeling of self-satisfaction stayed for a little while and then faded, but started to build again at the approach of Degree Day. Meriel took a keen interest and not just because of wondering what to wear; the university's Chancellor who was to present the degrees was a former opera singer of international renown. But more to the point, she had been at the same school as Meriel.

'My only claim to fame,' my wife told her friends. 'I stood next to Janet in choir practice and she sang and I opened and shut my mouth in time to the music.'

Degree Day was a grand occasion for dressing up and it felt unreal to be involved. The campus was heaving with students looking unusually kempt and accompanied by uneasy, self conscious parents. In the changing rooms, we all opened our boxes from the academic costumiers. I could not believe it: who was that strange figure in the mirror swishing around in hood and gown?

We emerged into the daylight in all our finery and everyone was taking photographs. As I wandered around it was fun to match the parents to the students. Girls whom I had seen grow into self-confident young ladies shyly introduced this elderly student in cap and gown to their puzzled parents.

One added by way of helpful explanation, 'John always kept things going in the seminars.'

'Oh yes,' said the parents, looking at me suspiciously, until I introduced Meriel and Penny and my respectability returned.

* * *

We gathered in the Central Hall sitting in rows in strict alphabetical order. I was next to the young man who had circled Anna when she was on the rebound from Richard. 'What did you get?' I whispered.

'A good solid Third,' he said and grinned.

'Anna got a First.'

'Don't I know it!'

I waved discreetly to Meriel and Penny as the long boring ceremony began.

Those receiving honorary degrees looked justifiably embarrassed as their sponsors extolled their virtues in speeches of incomprehensible, mind-blowing complexity. I suspected that the sponsoring lecturers thought this was their moment to glitter in front of the great and the good and they were going to take it.

With the eulogies completed it was the turn for us lesser mortals. Anna led off the parade of the English Literature graduates students by right of getting a First and having a surname beginning with A. She looked like a film star: head up, shoulders back and with a slow, measured walk. Someone should have shouted, 'Lights! Camera! Action!'

By the time they got to my letter of the alphabet the lady Chancellor was suffering from wrist fatigue and her duties were taken over by the Vice Chancellor. I was a little peeved about this; I had so looked forward to interrupting the smooth flow of the graduate production line by saying to the Chancellor, 'Hi there! You went to school with my wife.'

That would have broken up the routine, but the chance had gone. I joined the queue, waited for my name to be read out and carefully avoided the indignity of falling up the stage steps. I shook the Vice Chancellor by the hand.

Hurrah! Made it! I was now the proud owner of a little scroll of paper rolled up in a cardboard tube.

★ ★ ★

It was all over apart from the lunch where we were seated with no one we knew. I spotted Anna with her parents in another dining room and we gave each other a little wave. Her parents gave the impression of having strayed from some Embassy party and found themselves by accident in the workers' canteen.

We found Julien and chatted to his parents, but the social edginess was all pervasive: the students were subdued and on their best behaviour and the parents behaved like bemused aliens in a mysterious world.

People drifted about after lunch uncertain what to do, uncertain how to finally end it all. I showed Meriel and Penny some of the seminar rooms, for what purpose I could not imagine, and suddenly we came face to face with the Professor.

I introduced them. 'Your turn next,' he said to Meriel jovially. 'Get yourself enrolled and get yourself a degree, too.'

'Certainly not,' said Meriel firmly. 'Two clever-clogs in the family are quite enough, what with my daughter and him. I'll remain the happy cabbage.'

The Professor looked puzzled, but thankfully amused.

★ ★ ★

Meriel's patience throughout the day had been worthy of an archangel and so had Penny's. They clearly did not want to be the ones to bring the event to a close.

'Anything else you want us to see?' Meriel asked gently.

'No that's it.'

'Great day, Dad. I'm proud of you.'

We parted, they heading for the car park, and me for the changing rooms. I walked along the covered ways, my academic robe swishing about my knees and my board at a jaunty angle. And why not make the most of it? This would be the last time in my life that I could flaunt myself in such fine feathers.

By the pedestrian bridge three gowned figures were chatting and they turned and watched my approach with amusement.

'You look like a headmaster,' said Gareth laughing. He was the 'seriously clever' young man who had, as expected, achieved a starred First.

I tipped my mortarboard. 'And the best of luck to you, young sirs,' I said, assuming the role they had given me.

'And good luck to you, sir,' they said mockingly raising their mortar boards in salute.

★   ★   ★

Up on the pedestrian bridge, I saw Meriel and Penny down below walking towards the car park. I whistled and waved my mortar-board in the air. They didn't hear me. I had this idiotically sentimental idea of wanting them to see me like this, a solitary figure in my academic robes waving to them from the bridge, a last image of granddad's university days for them to remember. Oh this dreadful striving for immortality through captured memories.

They did not hear me and they did not see me, but I waved my mortar board at them just the same. If they did not remember this moment I most certainly would.

That was it. My university days were over. And now what . . . ?

★   ★   ★

I had always been envious of friends with Oxbridge degrees who on reading about someone famous in the newspaper commented with affected casualness, 'I was at King's with him.'

I got to wondering: if I lived long enough and my university contemporaries got a move on, might I, too, be able to boast about knowing someone famous?

Shu Lin, armed with her First Class degree: would she become a powerful media figure in Thailand? A revolutionary?

Gareth, I could see fast-tracking his way through the upper echelons of the Civil Service.

And what of Anna: Madam Ambassador, perhaps?

Tanya, I could see as a stroppy London councillor stirring up the social services department.

And Richard — a clever backroom boy beavering away somewhere in the city?

Julien? He was my great hope for fame by association. He had become a barrister and was aspiring to become an MP: a Government minister one day?

I had vivid memories of them all on Degree Day, full of enthusiasm and me in their midst looking, I suspected, faintly ridiculous in my cap and gown. They had all gone off full of 'get up and go' and left me behind fatally infected by their enthusiasm and wondering, to where am I going to 'get up and go'?'

★ ★ ★

Foolishly, I had thought that university would be something complete and satisfying of itself, but instead it had turned out to be an unsettling launch pad. The young ones had taken off and flung themselves at the four corners of the earth, eager to make their mark, leaving me behind them hesitant and mentally stirred up.

I concluded that two problems would have to be addressed in order to survive post-university. First, some very serious thought had to be given to my re-entry into normal domestic life. It had been anticipated that granddad, having had his little ego trip, would sink back into his easy chair and read seed catalogues. He would discuss holidays and house-painting not obscure ancient authors. Family and friends expected what they called 'normal conversations'.

In other words it was imperative that I became, as quickly as possible, the man that my wife said she had married. Cloud Nine had to be vacated as quickly as possible and residence resumed on planet earth; that I endeavoured to do.

And as I cut the lawn and half heartedly poked at the weeds I brooded on the second problem encapsulated in the simple question: what was I going to do now?

Mentally I was still on that launch pad ready to go, but where? Grandly describing my mood as one of 'divine discontent' was no help.

As I paced the lawn enlightenment came slowly . . .

'Tend your gardens,' Voltaire had said, when confronted with the very same problem.

And he was right, for pacing up and down the lawn led me to an answer. What was wrong with 'divine discontent', I told myself, as the lawnmower growled through the long grass. Discontent, divine or otherwise, provided the spur for finding its own cure.

I had a sudden memory of a spiky-haired hippy in a pink and white Andy Pandy suit. 'The quest is the thing, man!'

That was it! Everyone else had gone off on their quests so why should I not have a quest of my own? But what exactly?

Writing! It suddenly came to me that I had spent my life writing, so why stop now . . . All those books I had analysed and all those themes I had picked apart must have given me some new ideas.

Andy Pandy was with me again. 'Sometimes the journey is stationary, man.' How true and how useful for someone of my age. 'And the journey can be in your head, man.'

Right again, Andy boy!

My journey could indeed be stationary and in my head and what did it matter if my efforts never saw a library shelf. 'The quest is the thing, man!'

I daydreamed happily and the lawn mower shot into a flower bed . . .

Afterword

by
Graham Parry
Emeritus Professor of English
University of York

It is not easy being a student in your mid-sixties, entering a world largely populated by people two generations younger than you who have spent the last few years preparing themselves for university. Most older people who want the higher education that they missed when young opt for the Open University, or take up some of the offerings of U3A — the University of the Third Age — where there is a reasonable flexibility about the timetable and the requirements. But when John Scott entered the University of York to read English in 1990 he was taking on a full-scale degree course at a time when his private life was especially demanding. His wife was hoping for a more spacious life after his retirement, his daughter was expecting a child, and he had a lawn that endlessly needed mowing. Small wonder that a sense of pressure runs through this memoir, pressure of a quite different order from that experienced by the average undergraduate.

John's relationship with his fellow under-graduates forms one strong line of his narrative, as he becomes familiar with their problems and preoccupations. He listens to their views on the course, learns about their affairs, and on the advice of his wife, sensibly refrains from offering the wisdom of experi-ence from the vantage point of age. His presence is accepted without surprise by the students, and by the lecturers, and a *modus vivendi* begins to establish itself. Like passengers on a liner who must accept the same company for the duration, they get to know one another as an enjoyable three year voyage gets under way.

John soon finds that an English course at York contains a great deal that is not evidently English. There is Anglo-Saxon to be learnt, as well as Middle English, and there is an expectation that a student should know something of Greek drama, as well as Latin poetry. The Bible is incessantly invoked as a source and point of reference. The French course on Racine and Molière proves to be a trial between pleasure and pain. American literature is assumed to be an adjunct of English. How can one hold all this together, and make it all inter-relate? The answer is by incessant reading, intermittent thought, guidance from tutors and encouragement from fellow students.

John's reactions to the courses he takes form, for me, the centre of his account. He discovers that nothing is as straightforward as it seems. The surface meaning of a poem, a play or a novel may indeed be superficial: there are other layers of meaning beneath, some of them seemingly at odds with one's first impression. He is told early on by one lecturer to 'problematize' whatever he reads: but does this lead to enrichment or confusion? He finds lecturers themselves disagree about the merits of books they are presenting. Some tutors accept that there is a recognised canon of major works that should be read as the core of an English degree; others believe that we need to hear the voices excluded from the canon, and compensate for their long neglect. How does the student negotiate his way across a landscape full of conflicting signs? It is part of the mystery of the educational process that somehow, at the end of three years, some resolution is achieved.

As a member of the Department myself in those days, I am naturally intrigued to discover what John thought of the teaching he received. I am pleased to learn most of the lectures came over effectively, with plenty of interest and stimulus, and I can believe that there were occasions that were drear and dull. It is usually the lively lectures one remembers, of course. He catches the variety of lecturing styles on offer very credibly: I recognise many of the mannerisms and idiosyncrasies of my colleagues here. Long may such variety persist.

His experience of English seminars at York will strike a familiar note with hundreds of his contemporaries. Some seminars hit the ground running, others spark into life after a meandering start, and some limp along with students reluctant to speak or with the tutor oppressively dominant.

I would make the point here that John Scott was very fortunate to have been taught entirely by full-time members of staff throughout his degree course. That is no longer the case, at York and everywhere else. The priority that is now given to research and publication, rather than to teaching, because departmental funding depends on the publication record, means that many regular members of staff are away on research leave. Higher numbers of students also stretch the teaching capacity of the Department. In consequence, a good deal of undergraduate teaching is done by part-timers or by postdoctoral people. This significant change is the result of government policy towards universities, and in my view it is greatly to be deplored.

As an older student, John had to adjust to values and attitudes that are much different from those his generation accepted as the norm. John had to try to make sense of Critical Theory as he embarked on his course: a subject that hardly existed in his younger days, and a subject that bewilderingly supposes that the critic is more sophisticated and subtle than the author on whom he is commenting.

What comes across very strongly in his memoir is the difficulty he had in coming to terms with feminism, a movement that was reaching high tide in John's time. He is disconcerted by aggressive feminists he encounters, with their convictions that women writers have been sidelined by the male critics in academia. Their desire to correct the balance by over-emphasising the neglected merits of women writers, and their tendency to ignore the major male writers in favour of their female contemporaries have found a receptive audience among university students of English, who are these days predominantly young women. John would always have found himself in a male minority in lectures and seminars, and he was highly conscious of the strength of feminist feeling.

This memoir of an undergraduate career has a particular value as a record of university life in the 1990s. Although hundreds of thousands now attend university, detailed and thoughtful accounts of the experience are extremely rare. The interaction between John and the teenage students provides one eventful phase of the story, and the reactions of his wife to his unexpected new life form another. The pervasive theme is the growth of intellectual enlightenment as his understanding of literature deepens. As a former journalist on The Yorkshire Post, John has the writing skills needed to keep the narrative lively, and also well-developed powers of observation to provide the telling detail. The reader will come away convinced that higher education at any stage of life irradiates the mind and adds to the pleasures of consciousness. Who knows, the book may even encourage others to follow the path that John Scott has taken.

We do hope that you have enjoyed reading this large print book.

Did you know that all of our titles are available for purchase?

We publish a wide range of high quality large print books including:
Romances, Mysteries, Classics
General Fiction
Non Fiction and Westerns

Special interest titles available in large print are:
The Little Oxford Dictionary
Music Book
Song Book
Hymn Book
Service Book

Also available from us courtesy of Oxford University Press:
Young Readers' Dictionary
(large print edition)
Young Readers' Thesaurus
(large print edition)

For further information or a free brochure, please contact us at:
Ulverscroft Large Print Books Ltd.,
The Green, Bradgate Road, Anstey,
Leicester, LE7 7FU, England.
Tel: (00 44) 0116 236 4325
Fax: (00 44) 0116 234 0205

Other titles published by
The House of Ulverscroft:

FIRE SEASON

Philip Connors

For nearly a decade, Philip Connors has spent half of each year in a small room at the top of a tower, on top of a mountain, alone in millions of acres of remote American wilderness. His job: to look for wildfires. Capturing the wonder and grandeur of his work, *Fire Season* evokes the eerie pleasure of solitude and the majesty, might and beauty of untamed fire. Connors' time up on the peak is filled with drama — fires; spectacular midnight lightning storms and silent mornings, awakening above the clouds; surprise encounters with smokejumpers, black bears, and an abandoned, dying fawn.

WITNESS TO EVIL

Veronica McGrath

Veronica McGrath's story tells how her tyrannical mother coldly planned and executed the murder of her husband. As an innocent young girl, Veronica witnessed her father's brutal killing by her mother and her own fiance Colin Pinder. Her mother threatened to sign her into a psychiatric unit if she alerted the police. Veronica's beloved dad, Bernard, was the only stability she'd known. In 2010, her mother was sentenced to life imprisonment for murder, and her former partner was convicted of manslaughter. *Witness to Evil* is Veronica's account of her personal journey, and her fight to win justice for her father.

GIANT GEORGE

Dave Nasser with Lynne Barrett-Lee

In 2006, Dave and Christie Nasser bought a Great Dane puppy. They named him George and from a quivering misfit he grew into a gentle giant. In 2010, George was crowned by the Guinness Book of World Records as the Tallest Dog in the World, ever. He's appeared on Oprah and has his own global fan club. At five feet tall and seven feet long he is still a big softie, eager to play and boisterous to the point of causing chaos. *Giant George* is the heart-warming story of a much-cherished pet, who continues to make Dave and Christie happy.